ALONE
THROUGH
THE FORBIDDEN LAND

Gustav Krist was born in 1894 in the Meidling district of
Vienna. In the First World War he was captured on the
Eastern Front and imprisoned in various parts of the
Russian Empire, including Central Asia. Unable to settle
in peacetime Austria, he soon returned to the area and
embarked on the adventures recounted in this book. He
died in his native Vienna in 1937.

Fitzroy Maclean, former diplomat, soldier and politician,
is well known for his writings on Eastern Europe and the
former Soviet Union. His own journey through Soviet
Central Asia in the 1930s is described in his *Eastern
Approaches*, recently reissued by Penguin.

ALONE
THROUGH
THE FORBIDDEN LAND

Journeys in Disguise
through Soviet Central Asia

by
GUSTAV KRIST

with an introduction by
Fitzroy Maclean

Ian Faulkner Publishing
Cambridge · England

Ian Faulkner Publishing Ltd
Lincoln House
347 Cherry Hinton Road
Cambridge CB1 4DJ

First published in Austria in 1937
under the title *Allein durchs verbotene Land*
This translation first published in 1939
by Faber and Faber Ltd

This edition copyright © Ian Faulkner Publishing Ltd 1992
Introduction copyright © Fitzroy Maclean 1992

A CIP record for this book is available from the British Library.

ISBN 1-85763-011-4

Printed in Great Britain by Billings and Sons Ltd

Introduction

Not long after I had been posted to our Embassy in Moscow in February 1937 a German colleague gave me a copy of Gustav Krist's then newly published *Allein durchs verbotene Land*. It gripped my imagination. I had long fancied the idea of one day making Flecker's Golden Journey to Samarkand. Indeed, it was one reason why I had asked the Foreign Office to post me to Moscow, which struck me as being as good a jumping-off place for it as any. But now my mind was made up. It was just a question of how soon I could get there and what route I should follow. The fact that Soviet Turkestan had by then become even more of a forbidden zone than in Krist's day was, I must admit, an added attraction. Not even the all too likely prospect of picking up a *rishta* or guinea-worm, the then widely prevalent pest of which Krist gives such a lively description at the very start of his book, was enough to deter me. In those days I was young enough to be convinced that things like that could never happen to me. All I thought of in my enthusiasm was the moon rising over mosques and minarets and the caravans making their leisurely way across an endless expanse of desert.

Somehow, against all probability, I managed to get not only to Samarkand but to Bokhara, at that time even harder of access. And the day came when, having finally reached Bokhara, I passed on foot through the great gate of the city by the light of the rising moon and in the wake of a caravan of shambling Bactrian dromedaries snuffling and grunting down my neck. Rarely in life are one's youthful fancies so completely fulfilled. This time the reality surpassed my wildest dreams. That night Central Asia became an abiding interest.

How had Russian Turkestan come to be so universally regarded as a forbidden land? For centuries the formidable natural barrier of deserts and mountains which blocked the approaches to it, coupled with the notorious ferocity and fanaticism of its inhabitants and their rulers, served to put off all but the most intrepid of travellers. And for the few who reached it the chances of ever leaving it alive were frankly minimal. Which of course made it for some all the more of a challenge.

Then, in the nineteenth century, Central Asia was the scene of what came to be called the Great Game. Here the rival interests of the British and Russian empires overlapped and conflicted. Brave men risked their lives on improbable missions to the courts of exotic tyrants who made the best use they could of the opportunity thus offered to play one great power off against the other. More than once actual war seemed likely but in the event prudence prevailed.

By the time Gustav Krist reached Central Asia, things were different. The First World War (in which Great Britain and Imperial Russia were allies) and the Russian Revolution of 1917 changed the situation completely. The journey Krist describes in *Through the Forbidden Land* was in fact his second visit to Central Asia. He had first been taken there in 1916 as an Austrian prisoner of war and, having escaped, stayed on, like his fellow prisoner and compatriot Feldwebel Josip Broz (later Marshal Tito), for several years, making himself useful to the inhabitants in one way or another.

What is remarkable is that Krist, having returned to his native Austria from Central Asia in 1922, should immediately have felt the urge to go back there. Though by now in gainful employment in neighbouring Persia, he readily threw it all up and used every stratagem to get back across the frontier he had recently crossed in the opposite direction. Turkestan, it could truly be said, had stolen his wits away.

Krist's account of his experiences once across the frontier is in itself fascinating, for Central Asia is and has always been a fascinating place. What makes it of particular interest at the present time is that once again the whole region is in a state of flux. Even more than in Krist's day it is currently impossible to say with any degree of certainty what the future holds for an area twice the size of Europe.

In 1924 the Soviet Union (which fell apart at the end of 1991) had just officially come into being, though Lenin, its creator, was by then already dead. After a brief period of independence under their former rulers, the Emir of Bokhara and the Khan of Khiva, the Central Asian republics had, despite fairly strong resistance, mostly from the mullahs, been brought back into the Russian fold. But at this stage they were being ridden on a much looser rein than later. For a time, as Krist tells us, there was even a certain amount of give and take, and Communism and Islam existed side by side. Not until after 1929 did Stalin's rule become totalitarian.

By the time I reached Soviet Central Asia in 1937, a dozen years after Krist, Moscow's hold was already much tighter, but still not complete enough for the Soviet Government to dare take any chances. Memories of armed nationalist resistance, of Enver Pasha and the Basmatchis, were still fresh. Foreigners were more rigorously excluded than ever, and in March 1938 I myself saw Faisullah Khojayev, an old Bolshevik and a hero of the Revolution in Central Asia, condemned to death in Moscow as a bourgeois nationalist traitor.

In the years that followed the Second World War, the Soviet Union, a now victorious superpower, felt secure enough to open Central Asia to the outside world. Samarkand and Bokhara, by this time safely sanitised, were crowded with foreign tourists. Having supposedly achieved its object, the anti-God campaign against Islam abated and some of the once ubiquitous anti-God museums were actually shut down. Meeting the Grand Mufti of Central Asia, you quickly realised that, like the high dignitaries of the Orthodox Church, he had long since done a deal with the regime. But, as so often in the East, things were not always what they seemed. The forty million professing Moslems claimed by the Mufti were not all phoneys. Visiting the Shakhi-i-Zindeh in Samarkand, now no longer an anti-God museum, you constantly encountered pious pilgrims worshipping at its sacred shrines. Nor was it possible to leave out of account the hundreds of devout Moslems who thronged the mosques on Friday or the quiet little groups of turbaned worshippers of whom you caught a glimpse prostrating themselves in the privacy of their own courtyards.

There can be no doubt whatever that more than seventy years after the Bolshevik Revolution the Moslem religion and Moslem way of life have not only survived but have a big part to play in Central Asia. In the light of what is happening there today and of what is liable to happen there in the future, Gustav Krist's book is much more than a good read. It casts a revealing light on a part of the world which has been of considerable importance in the past and seems bound to become so again.

Fitzroy Maclean
Strachur, May 1992

ALONE
THROUGH
THE FORBIDDEN LAND

Journeys in Disguise
through Soviet Central Asia

by

GUSTAV KRIST

translated by

E. O. Lorimer

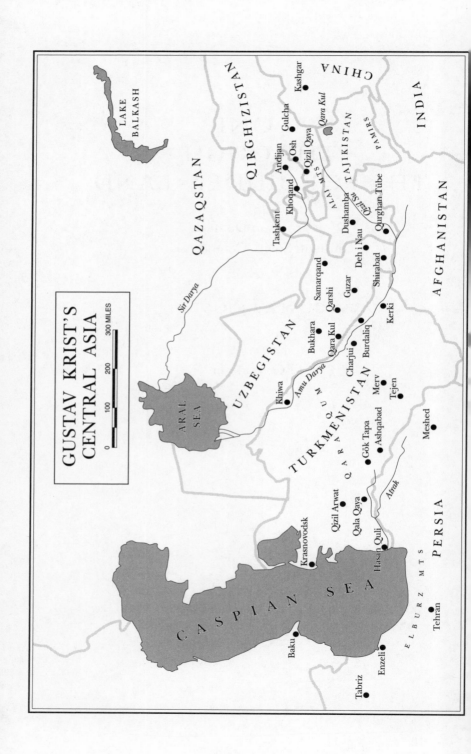

GUSTAV KRIST'S
CENTRAL ASIA

0   100   200   300 MILES

Translator's Note

The transliteration of place-names and vernacular words is a problem of great complexity. The most authoritative maps, based on the Survey of India, the War Office, and the Royal Geographical Society's maps, and the best foreign sources, are frequently at variance with each other and often inconsistent with themselves.

Since the majority of Central Asian place-names are significant – Red Water ('Qizil Su' in Turki and 'Surkh Ab' in Persian), Rock Fortress ('Tash Qurghan'), etc. – I have endeavoured to use such forms as would correctly indicate their original meaning, consulting for this purpose Redhouse for Turkish, Raquette for Turki, Steingass and Phillott for Persian, and in general the *Encyclopaedia of Islam*.

I am also deeply indebted for advice to my friend, Professor Vladimir Minorsky of London University, who is a European authority not only on Persian and Turkish but also on the geography of Central Asia.

In the case of names like Tashkent, Meshed, etc., which are well established in English usage, I have (inconsistently, but I trust acceptably) retained the familiar forms.

For fear of bewildering the casual reader I have not usually marked the long vowels of foreign words nor inserted the signs expressing the *'ain* or *hamza* of the Arabic script, nor attempted to render the subtleties of the Turki vowel system. The list of vernacular words at the end of the book will supply the clue to most of the significant place-names.

It may be pertinent to mention, for those not conversant with oriental languages, that the difference in pronunciation between *q* and *k* is roughly similar to the difference between the English *k*-sounds in 'calf' and 'king' respectively, though in Arabic itself the sound denoted by English *q* is pronounced much deeper in the throat than the *c* of the English 'calf'.

E. O. LORIMER

Preface

Year by year sportsmen and scientists travel in numbers through Africa, Australia, South America, and the islands of the South Seas, while Central Asia still remains almost unknown. The reasons for this state of affairs are various and many. The Amirate of Bukhara, the Kingdom of Afghanistan, the Khanate of Khiwa and the Russian territories in Turkistan have been almost completely closed to Europeans. Inhospitable deserts and mountains make scientific journeys exceptionally difficult and unfruitful. Since the World War such journeys have been impossible in Russian territory. During the War the Russian Government refused on political grounds to permit any European to enter Turkistan, and the Soviets are even more scrupulous than the Tsarist regime to keep Turkistan closed to foreigners.

Bukhara is a state about three times the size of Austria. Until 1917 it was more or less loosely a dependency of Russia; when in that year it successfully shook off the Russian yoke it forbade any European to cross its frontiers. In the summer of 1920 Red troops bombarded and occupied the capital, and the fugitive Amir took refuge with relatives in Afghanistan. The new constitutions of the three autonomous states, Uzbegistan, Tajikistan, and Turkmenistan hermetically sealed their borders, and the entry of a European was more sternly forbidden than ever before; even Russian travellers required a special permit.

Such Europeans as had visited Bukhara before the end of the nineteenth century were for the most part agents of the British, French, or Russian governments, who travelled either in disguise

5

or under the pretext of scientific research. They seldom returned. They were usually discovered and executed, or compelled to serve as slaves. The few among them who got back to Europe confided little concerning their adventures or experiences to the public, since as military emissaries it was their business to furnish reports only to their respective governments.

As early as 1243 an Englishman, Cooley, reached Bukhara. He was followed in 1271 by the Italian, Marco Polo, who lived at the court of Timur the Lame (Tamerlane). A hundred and thirty years elapsed before Clavigo's visit in 1403. Another two hundred years passed before the two Englishmen, Stell and Crofter, saw Bukhara in 1604. During the eighteenth and nineteenth centuries a number of Russian spies were successful in penetrating the country, and a handful of western Europeans, among whom were Vambéry, Schwarz, Lansdell, and Chanikoff; finally the two Englishmen, Stoddart and Conolly were executed in Bukhara in 1842. These were of course not the only travellers who attempted the journey, but most of the others failed to reach their goal, for the rivals Britain and Russia would inform the amirs in time of the plucky adventurers' intentions, and they were either detected and turned back at the frontiers, or taken prisoners to the capital, whence they were repatriated, after lengthy negotiations, in return for a heavy ransom – without having been allowed to see anything of Bukhara itself. It is characteristic of the country and its government that less than fifty years ago Russia had to redeem a number of her citizens out of Bukharan slavery.

In the early twentieth century a few men, Russians and British for the most part, succeeded in gaining entry to the country and endeavoured mutually to supplant each other in the favour of the Amir; for the governments of both countries looked on Bukhara as the heart of the Muslim world – which in fact it is to-day – and were seeking there a base for the penetration and conquest of Central Asia. For the moment the Russians have won the round.

It is now merely a matter of time – and no long time – till the Soviets will have so completely altered the face of Central Asia that

there will remain no memorial of the ancient empire of Timur save
a few ruined buildings and scanty literary records. In mentioning
Europeans in Bukhara I must not forget my fellow countryman,
the Austrian Russmann, who was taken prisoner by the Russians
during the War, escaped from Ashqabad, and became a cavalry
general. During the War there were some forty Austrians in
Bukharan service. I visited the country for the first time during the
War and had the good fortune to get to know the old Bukhara —
one of the most interesting countries in the world. To prevent
misapprehension, I here explicitly state that the travels I am about
to tell of make no pretence of having been undertaken in the
interests of science. Nothing but a love of adventure incited me to
force my way into a forbidden land in order to see more of it than
had been possible on my previous travels. In this spirit I commend
my book to the reader.

GUSTAV KRIST

Contents

Illustrations

11

I

A Bathing Trip and its Consequences

At the beginning of 1922 I came home from Turkistan. I had not been in Austria since 1914 and my prospects of being able to make a livelihood seemed bleak, for I found it hard to adapt myself to altered circumstances. At the end of the year I went out again to Persia and took service with a carpet merchant of Tabriz, in whose company I travelled through the whole length and breadth of the country.

For days my employer, Abul Qasim Qannadi, and I, with Qannadi's two servants, had been climbing steadily on our shaggy ponies through the ancient beech forests of the Elburz mountains. Some 7,800 feet above the sea we reached the watershed and began the descent towards the Caspian, which in that clear atmosphere gleamed blue in the light of the sun. We rejoiced that the day of our entry into Barfurush was near and that we should soon taste the last of the *mast* – the thick, boiled goat's milk which we bought from the mountain herdsmen – and revel in good mutton and fresh drinking water. For days past we had talked of little else than the delights of the week's rest which we promised ourselves in Barfurush. According to Qannadi, Barfurush was the Shiraz of north-east Persia, a town where milk and honey flowed in streams. I had by now some experience of Qannadi's enthusiasms and imagined that I could estimate the attractions of the place fairly correctly. When at last we rode into the miserable little mud town, however, I had to acknowledge with a shudder that I had after all been over-optimistic.

The Chief of Police was a personal friend of Qannadi's. We

13

pitched our felt tents in his garden and went off to the bazaar to
raise some provisions. Drought and bad harvests had prevailed
through the whole province of Mazandaran. The bazaar was dead.
I paid a lot of money for a few pomegranates, the only kind of fruit
available. There was no green fodder for the cattle so neither milk
nor cheese was to be had. After much inquiry here and there I
succeeded in buying a couple of dozen eggs. All the water in
Barfurush being brackish and full of dirt, I boiled it before drinking,
a procedure which astonished Qannadi. On the third day of our
stay I decided to ride to Meshed i Sar to get a bathe in the Caspian.
The twenty-seven- or twenty-eight-mile ride did not deter me,
for I hoped to be able to catch some fish which would form a
welcome addition to our spartan and monotonous menu. I told
Qannadi that I only wanted to bathe, which rendered him speech-
less with amazement. The idea that any one would ride twenty-
seven miles in this heat for the sake of a bathe . . . !

I trotted out of Barfurush before the sun was up, so as to escape
the fierce heat of midday. The temperature was well nigh unbear-
able in Barfurush, but it was a good twenty degrees hotter in
Meshed i Sar, for the shore boasts no vegetation of any kind
whatever. The miserable mud hovels stand in the middle of the
white sand of the seashore, which reflects the heat of the sun with
redoubled intensity. The only alleviation was the clear mountain
stream flowing down from the Elburz, on the bank of which the
chai-khana-ji had erected his little tea-house. After I had had my
bathe I bent a bit of rusty wire into a fish-hook and waded with it
far out into the shallow sea. As I caught the fish, I threaded them
on a string round my neck until I had as many as I wanted.

When I got back to the tea-shop I asked them to roast the fish
for me on their little charcoal fire and while waiting I dozed happily
on the bank of the stream. Far out at sea a tiny sailing-boat could
be seen bearing in our direction. An hour later four Turkomans
came into the tea-shop. In spite of the heat they were still wearing
their fur caps and camel-hair cloaks. From their conversation with
the host I gathered that they were coming from Chikishlar on the

Turkistan coast and were making for Enzeli with a cargo of melons and sheep's cheese. How poor these folk must be to face the hardships of a journey of three hundred miles or so in their primitive little craft in order to sell a few hundred melons and a few batman of cheese! They might have to wait for weeks in Enzeli before they could find a cargo to take back to Turkistan, so they would often be months away from home.

While he was talking to them, the *chai-khana-ji* frequently pointed to me. At last one of the Turkomans got up and came towards me. He obviously took every European for a doctor and asked if I could help him; he had terrible pains in his back. I had often dabbled in doctoring when need arose, so I said I must first see the sore place and asked him to take his clothes off.

If I hadn't taken it into my head to bathe at Meshed i Sar, or if the Turkoman had not been ill, this book would never have been written. I solemnly disclaim all responsibility for it. The guilt lies with the Turkoman Shir Dil, the Lion-Hearted – or more exactly with the horrible *rishta* he was unwillingly harbouring. I at once diagnosed the presence of a guinea-worm (*filaria mendinensis*) and as I had myself suffered twice from the brutes, I knew what to do. I removed the rude poultice of sheep's dung that covered a ghastly sore which must have been causing him agony. I asked Shir Dil if he had ever been in Bukhara. Yes, he said, four months ago he had been there on a visit to his brother-in-law in Hazrat Bashir. I had once had a guinea-worm in my thumb and once in my neck; but I had never before seen such a giant specimen, nor one so filthy and neglected.

The *rishta* is a typical Bukharan plague, which I have never met elsewhere.[1] It is caused by a worm two or three yards long and about a sixteenth of an inch thick. It breeds in water and the microscopic larva is swallowed when drinking. It works its way out to the subcutaneous tissue and causes ugly suppurating wounds. The guinea-worm thrives in the stagnant waters of Bukhara, in

1 See note, p. 221.

tanks and *ariqs*. Its inside contains a milky white liquid composed of an immense number of minute larvae scarcely visible to the naked eye. The worm divides in the water to let the young ones free and the larva-liquid spreads. If the infected water is drunk the larva enters the body, develops, and within a few months works its way out towards the surface.

I took a razor-blade, which I fortunately had with me in my saddle-bag, and begged Lion-Heart to show himself worthy of his name and bear the coming pain as best he could. Then I made an incision, and scarcely had the sharp instrument pierced the skin than a thick stream of black blood and pus gushed out over my hands. With my penknife I cut a splinter from one of the posts of the veranda and made a narrow slit in it. I then pressed the edges of the wound cautiously together and saw that my diagnosis had been correct, for a quarter of an inch of worm was exposed. I speedily inserted its head into the cleft of my small piece of wood. As you must wind the beast out by very slow degrees so as not to break it off – if you do, the patient is done for – the treatment was clearly going to take several days. I explained the case to Shir Dil's friends, who were sitting round, and begged them to give a couple of careful turns to the little stick every two hours. They promised to do this. I myself would come back the day after tomorrow from Barfurush to see my patient. I then bought a bundle of dried fish from the *chai-khana-ji* and started back.

As promised, I turned up in Meshed i Sar two days later. The patient was in good form and in the highest spirits; he was free from pain and overwhelmed me with thanks. The worm had already dried up so much that I was able cautiously to draw the rest of it completely out. I then washed the wound with alcohol and bandaged it up. The Turkomans fetched melons and cheese from their boat. Their excellent and juicy watermelons were a welcome treat such as I had not enjoyed for a long time.

The sight of the Turkomans re-awakened old memories of the years I had spent in Turkistan and Bukhara. I longed to see those countries once more and I decided to let Qannadi go on by himself to Asterabad and Jurjan, while I made a detour by Bukhara. I very much wanted to see what the country was like, now that it was the autonomous republic, Uzbegistan, of the Soviet Union. The Bukhara that I knew had been an independent state under its own Amir. It had been forced to permit Russian soldiers in its frontier towns, but had successfully prevented the entry of any European into the Holy City itself. Only my earlier friendship with the Beg of Kerki, who had later become the Amir's Qush Begi or Chief Minister, had opened the gates of the city to me.

I now questioned the four Turkomans about present conditions in Turkistan and Bukhara. They gladly told me all they knew, and when the time came to bid them good-bye I asked whether they would be willing to take me with them in their boat to Enzeli, so that I might procure a passport from the Soviet Russian Consul there permitting me to travel in the new republics. The grateful Turkomans welcomed the proposal with delight and promised to wait a few days till I should return again from Barfurush.

Everything that I did, or didn't do, during the two years I travelled with Qannadi hither and thither through Persia had been a source of ever-fresh surprise to him. On this occasion, however, speech failed him when I said that the Turkomans and the guinea-worm together had awakened old memories that called me irresistibly, and that I proposed starting for Enzeli the day after next in their little sailing-boat. When the words came back I had to listen till far into the night to his reproaches. I was an ungrateful dog, leaving my benefactor in the lurch. He would be delighted to hear that the wild Bukharans had murdered me or that the Bolsheviks had flung me into the worst dungeon in Bukhara.

Next morning, however, he helped me to pack my kit and wrote me a cheque for 300 tumans on the Enzeli branch of the National Bank of Persia. I asked him for the money because he had kindly been taking charge of my savings for me. He then adjured me not to be absent longer than a month at most, by which time he would be once more making for his home in Tabriz. If I did not catch him in Tehran I should go on ahead to Tabriz. The

17

good fellow little guessed how long it would be before we met again!

I took a servant with me to Meshed i Sar, handed my horse over to him, and put my scanty baggage on board the boat. The wind was favourable as we set sail for the west, and before long the little port had vanished from our sight.

We had passed Langrud and were approaching Resht one day, when Shir Dil's brother Khores relieved me of the fishing line. He flung out the hook, fastened the horsehair line round his right foot, and leaned back sleepily to take his ease. Suddenly there was a sharp tug at the line and Khores began to haul in with all his might. It was clear that an outsize fish had taken the bait. I hastened to his help and saw the head of a gigantic sturgeon rise out of the water. Good-bye to hook and tackle! We could never hope to get the enormous brute into our little boat. Khores pulled for all he was worth, the fish dived for its life. Khores, as the wiser of the two, yielded a little, but slipped and plopped into the sea – with the line still wound round his leg. His brother and Abdullah tore off their cloaks and leaped in after him. For the first time in my life I saw Turkomans swimming – and maybe those chaps didn't know what they were about! When they brought Khores to the surface again he was unconscious. I dragged him into the boat, opened his shirt and listened to his heart. It was still beating, but slowly and irregularly. With Shir Dil's help I got him out of his clothes and turned him over on his face. A jet of water shot out of his mouth. Then I turned him on his back again and began to try artificial respiration.

This procedure was entirely new to the Turkomans, and they watched me attentively. For more than a quarter of an hour I worked his arms up and down, till the sweat was streaming down my body, but Khores remained unconscious. At last his lips opened and I was overjoyed to see that his lungs were beginning to work regularly again. My *rishta* operation had won the hearty thanks of the Turkomans, but they now overwhelmed me with boundless gratitude for saving Khores' life. The proud Yomut, who had up till now considered me simply as their equal, suddenly developed a new feeling of respect. After the resuscitation of Khores, I was 'Tura' – Sir and Master.

Next day we sighted the pointed tongue of land on which Enzeli – nowadays rechristened Pahlavi – is situated. A few light gunboats and floating tanks were lying in harbour bringing oil from Baku for the men-of-war. Though Enzeli lies on the Persian coast, it was at that time still Russian territory, just as the port of Zara on the Dalmatian coast belongs to Italy. I went to the 'Hôtel Paris', which bore more resemblance to a tumble-down cowshed than to an hotel. I there booked the best room, whose sole furniture was a rickety chair and a bug- and louse-ridden bed. The chair also served the purpose of washstand, so I had to lift down an earthen basin weighing about half a hundredweight and put it on the floor whenever I wanted to sit down.

As soon as I had washed and shaved I dug out the Russian consul and expounded my project to him. I should like to travel by the next steamer via Baku to Krasnovodsk and from there to Samarqand. While I was talking the consul quietly drank one cup of tea after another, and bit little lumps off a sugarloaf, which he skilfully gripped in his front teeth, sucking his tea up through them. When I had finished he looked at me and said only the one word: 'Forbidden!'

Lengthy cross-examination extracted the information from him that entry into Turkistan from whatever point, for whatever reason, was on political grounds absolutely forbidden to any foreigner. Even Russians from the interior of the empire must arm themselves with a special permit from the Political Department, and such permits were only granted in exceptional cases.

In vain I reminded him that in 1922 Colin Ross crossed over from Baku and traversed Turkistan from end to end. He admitted that this was true. He had himself seen and spoken to Mr. Ross on that occasion, but that gentleman had had a special permit from Moscow, and even so he had not been allowed to move a single step to right or left of the Central Asian railway line. An official of the Cheka had accompanied Mr. Ross and never left his side, and his instructions were immediately to arrest the stranger if he attempted to quit the railway.

I then asked whether Khidiralieff, a personal friend of mine, who was now chairman of the Central Executive of Turkistan, could not procure me a permit in Tashkent. The consul said no; not even Comrade Khidiralieff could issue a permit; only Moscow was empowered to do this. I professed incredulity, since Uzbegistan was now an autonomous republic and therefore her internal affairs must be independent of Russia. The consul had bitten off a new piece of sugar, and he almost choked himself as he burst into a loud laugh over this ingenuous argument.

'You really must not be so childish, Tovarish!' he said. 'The Turkistan comrades are autonomous just as long as it suits us, and just to the extent that seems desirable. Get this crazy journey out of your head. Take my word for it, you will never reach Bukhara. And what on earth do you want to do there, anyway? It is just a country like any other – no better, no worse. Now let's be friends. Will you take a glass of tea with me?'

After tea I went down to the customs harbour to find the boat with my Turkoman friends and tell them my ill luck. With one voice they offered to take me with them and land me on the coast of Turkistan. I could go ashore unnoticed, and once I had got a few miles into the desert not a soul would worry further about me. There was much to be said for this plan, but it seemed to me a shade too risky. I knew something of summary Russian justice. Once already I had almost faced a firing-squad. I might not get off a second time. To enter forbidden Turkistan without papers? I would sooner pay a call on the Devil and his mother-in-law in Hell.

The thought of going to Bukhara despite the Russians was, however, so enticing, that I could not banish it from my mind. How often had I had the words 'impossible' and 'forbidden' hurled at me – and yet got my own way in the end? Why should I not pull it off once again?

For a long time I pondered the alternatives. At last I remembered that I had a friend in Qizil Arwat who might be able to help me. I must get into touch with him as soon as might be. The Austrian ex-prisoner of war, Steinschneider, had got naturalised and had settled there. He and I had, for years, been fellow prisoners in Fort Alexandrovsk and in Samarqand. As a Russian citizen Stein-schneider was sure to have lots of papers; if only I could borrow some from him I would risk the journey to Bukhara. If he were still alive, and if he were still in Qizil Arwat, I knew he would be ready and willing to see me through.

I must send a letter to Steinschneider by a safe hand. Quickly I made up my mind and turned to Khores: 'Khores, would you be willing to go from Chikishlar to Qizil Arwat to look up a friend of mine?' 'Yes, sir!' he said. Khores said this 'Yes' as briefly and simply as if I had asked him to walk across a street, instead of making a journey of two hundred and twenty miles or so across the Khan-baghi Qum Desert and back.

I then arranged with the Turkomans that I should accompany them back as far as Mahmudabad — still on the Persian coast, somewhat west of Barfurush — and wait there with the Forest Officer, an Austrian compatriot, until Khores should bring me Steinschneider's answer.

A week later our preparations were so far advanced that we were able to sail. The ship had loaded up with charcoal for *manqals*. A *manqal* is a little basin to hold burning charcoal which the nomads place under their padded quilts to keep their feet warm in winter. It is the only heating apparatus which they possess to mitigate the savage cold of the desert, for in spite of its enormous area the whole of western Turkistan is devoid of timber. In the oases there are chenar trees and black elm, but these are so valuable and so essential to life that they must not be felled, and the indispensable charcoal must be brought often for hundreds of miles on camel-back from Farghana or from the Bukhara mountains. The nomads who live on the coasts of the Caspian, or who touch it in their wanderings, have therefore for decades been wont to fetch their

21

charcoal from the Persian shores, much to the injury of the forests in the Elburz.

Meantime I had again looked up the consul. He said he thought I was quite mad, for no sane man would set out to cross the deserts unless he had to.

I had, however, been born with a thick skull. When I said good-bye to the consul I was more than ever determined to cross the forbidden frontiers.

We sailed from Enzeli at dawn, steering for the mouth of the Qizil Uzen, after which we intended to hug the coast. A favouring wind brought us on the fourth day to Mahmudabad. Amul lies not far inland from this point and an Austrian, Moser, was acting as forest officer there, in the employ of the Persian Government. Khores was to find me there when he came back. The Turkomans again set sail for the open sea. I stood on the shore for a long time till their sails disappeared on the horizon. Should I ever see them again? Everything depended on what answer Khores would bring.

My kit had been dumped on the sand. I walked into Mahmu-dabad to hire a horse for the ride to Amul. On arrival I was received with open arms by Herr Moser, and I should like to take this opportunity to thank him most warmly for his unstinted hospitality and wise advice. I stayed three weeks with this remarkable man and gained an insight into local conditions which I should otherwise have sought in vain. There is only one thing I can never forgive him. On every single one of my twenty-three days he dragged his most reluctant guest to hunt panther. Not one panther did I see, alive or dead, though the herdsmen and charcoal-burners again and again protested that they had seen the spoor of a full-grown panther within the last few days.

We were after panther again and had climbed close on 3,500 feet. It had rained hard the preceding day and at every step we sank to the ankles in clay and mud. I had slipped and fallen at least a score of times and was covered with mud from head to foot and thoroughly miserable. At noon I suggested that we should turn home. When we got back to Moser's house in Amul, there was a Turkoman sitting at the entrance door. It was Khores.

'Have you got a letter, Khores?'

'I have, sir!'

He answered, 'I have,' as calmly as if he had brought an answer from next door.

Hastily I tore open the envelope. It contained a long letter from Steinschneider with the assurance that he would do everything humanly possible for me. He enclosed a pass from the Soviet of Qizil Arwat granting Ferdinand Steinschneider permission to make his permanent residence in Bukhara and Turkistan.

My hopes had not deceived me. I replaced his photograph by one of my own.

Nothing now stood between me and the forbidden land. I decided to start at once.

When towards midnight we reached Mahmudabad and our boat, Shir Dil and his friends gave me a hearty welcome. I had scarcely taken my seat and stowed my kit before they had weighed anchor and hoisted sail. The light-laden vessel shot like an arrow through the waves. Shir Dil explained that they were heading due north so as not to fall foul of the Russian warships, which had their base in the Bay of Ashur-ada – also Persian territory. The warships along the coast were wont to develop an unhealthy curiosity, especially at night, and sweep the sea with their searchlights to catch smuggling vessels or any fugitives from the Russian paradise.

We held our course due north until midday, then we tacked steadily towards land, keeping in about the same latitude. It was pitch dark when we came within reach of land, and the boat sailed into the Hasan Quli Bay, where the Atrak flows into the Caspian. I was terribly afraid we should be subject to some sort of inspection here. The Turkomans reassured me. The control boat had left the bay some hours ago and the native fishermen didn't bother their heads about any one. We sailed up the bay for a good four hours, and in spite of a favouring wind we were making slower and slower progress. When I pointed this out to Khores he told me that we

23

had left the mouth of the Atrak far behind us and for more than an hour had been working upstream against the current.

Quite suddenly night changed to morning, and I saw that we were sailing the waters of a muddy, yellow desert river. The banks were absolutely flat and level, as if the Atrak were an artificial canal. As far as the eye could see there was nothing round us but the greyish yellow of the desert sand, broken here and there by a few leafless saksaul bushes (*Anabasis ammodendron*). Towards midday we came to a sharp bend in the river and Khores pointed into the desert on our left. Trees and houses could just be discerned in the distance and I learned that we were approaching the frontier fort of Yaghli Olum, where the Atrak forms the boundary between Persia and Russian Turkistan. The helmsman steered straight for the bank, where a number of other boats of various sizes already lay at anchor. Not a human being was in sight. We might have crossed the Styx and found ourselves in the country of the dead.

We jumped ashore and set out for the standing camp of my Turkoman friends. Khores would come along next day with camels and fetch our goods and the boat's gear. Shir Dil assured me that the stuff might lie there for weeks or months and no one would steal so much as a cooking pot or a match. Such is the respect which the sons of the desert pay to other people's property – unless they are actually out on a raiding party.

II

Guest of the Yomut Turkomans

W̲e had tramped for an hour through the sand when we came to a dip in the ground and halted. Green fields spread out before us interspersed with numerous fruit gardens, tall silver poplars and chenar trees, amongst which nestled the brown walls of the Turkomans' low mud huts and the black felt walls of their tents. Camels, horses, and donkeys were grazing over stretches of scanty grass. We had reached Qala-Qaya, the standing camp or village of the Yomut.

In contrast to the other women of Turkistan, the Turkoman women go about unveiled and do not take flight at the approach of a strange man. The two brothers took me along first to their father's tent. Alim Qul had formerly been the all-powerful Khan of Gök Tapa, which had offered the longest and most embittered resistance to the Russian conquest of Turkistan. For nearly a year the fort had been vainly besieged by General Skobeleff. After it was taken the chief was banished and all the survivors of the town had followed him into exile and founded themselves a new home on a small tributary of the Atrak.

The news of the brothers' arrival with a strange *urus* – 'Russian', as any European is called – spread like lightning through the encampment, and when I stepped towards the door of Alim Qul's yurt I saw a fine old man in picturesque Yomut costume sitting before the tent. He was at least six foot six, and his tall, white shaggy hat made him seem even more. Uncannily shrewd, wide-awake eyes scanned the intruder. There was a peculiar power in his glance and I could easily understand that his subjects obeyed this man without question, even when he sent thousands of them to their death. For several seconds the inexorable eyes rested on me as if they would read my very soul. Meantime a hundred men, women, and children had gathered round.

Shir Dil stepped forward, bowed deeply to his father, and said: 'Father, I bring our brother to you, the man of whom I have told you so much, who saved the life of both your sons.'

The old man nodded, stood up and threw both his arms round me, clapping me on the back with his right hand. He thus created me the official guest of the camp, and I was now more securely guarded than by a regiment of soldiers. Turkoman hospitality is unexampled and unlimited. However great his poverty, the Turkoman will slaughter his last sheep for his guest, even though the guest be a despised Unbeliever. He will not only give him his last crust but he will at need defend him at the risk of his own life — even against his own relations and tribal brothers. The rights of hospitality are inviolable. The person of a stranger who commits a theft, or even a murder, in his host's house, is sacred as long as he remains within the house or camp. Pursuit may not be taken up until the miscreant is out of sight.

Many other dwellers in the *aul* had built themselves houses of reeds and mud, but Alim Qul had preferred to make himself a court consisting of several yurts. He wanted to live and die in the surroundings in which he had been born and which are still those of tens of thousands of his race.

Alim Qul accompanied me to the guest tent, where his eldest granddaughter served me with *nan* and *chai*, namely flaps of bread and tea. This latter is green Indian tea to which salt and mutton fat have been added. Such a form of hospitality is usual amongst the Turkomans and Qirghiz, but a stranger amongst the Sarts, Uzbegs, or Bukharans would never be permitted to set eyes on the women-folk of his host's household. How profoundly the teachings of Communism have modified these traditional customs I was to discover later.

The yurt assigned to me was a magnificent specimen of its kind.

The floor and the walls were covered with glorious old Turkoman rugs – which Europe erroneously calls 'Bukhara carpets'. I thought of my friend and employer, Qannadi, and how his eyes would jump out of his head if he could see these magnificent rugs. The nights were already very cold and in the centre of the room stood a beautiful copper *manqal* full of charcoal, the fumes and smoke of which were allowed to escape through an opening in the roof of the yurt. A number of padded quilts and cushions were also provided, while a *chilim* (hubble-bubble) and two hammered brass water-pots completed the equipment.

Next evening I was invited to the Khan's tent; it was much less luxurious than the guest tent. Thick felt carpets covered the floor, a few plain hubble-bubbles stood about, and two brass water-pots for hand-washing; simple carpets hung on the walls and in front of them a whole arsenal of various weapons: guns, daggers, clubs, bows and arrows, blow-pipes, curved sabres, and pistols, as well as a quite modern Colt revolver.

A princely meal was brought in large brass basins. Rich cuts off the breast of a fat-tailed sheep had been roasted in my honour, and a mountain of this meat was piled in front of my place. It was followed by large fishes roasted on a spit; next came the much-prized *airan*, a mixture of sour camel's, goat's and mare's milk. Since spoons are unknown and everything has to be eaten with the fingers, I left my own spoon hidden in my boot and tried to imitate the procedure of my hosts so as not to hurt their feelings. Innumerable cups of *chai i shirin*, or sweetened tea, formed the final course.

Next day the whole tribe celebrated my coming. All the young men of the *aul*, mounted on their magnificent Turkoman ponies, assembled between the camp and the river Atrak. The old men brought me a horse and I rode out with them to see a *baigha*. Shir Dil had thoughtfully explained the whole proceeding to me the day before and I was thus enabled promptly to offer a prize of ten Persian tumans.

The Khan was carrying a newly-slaughtered sheep on the saddle in front of him. A boy then dragged the carcass two hundred yards or so out into the desert. The chief gave a shout and the riders dashed off in a wild gallop towards where the sheep was lying on the sand.

The point of the *baigha* is this: the riders try to lift the sheep off the ground and bring it back to the Khan. No sooner had one horseman secured the sheep than a dozen others hurled themselves on him, endeavouring to snatch it from him. In a moment or two the wild hunt was completely hidden in a cloud of dust and sand, while men and horses wrestled together in a savage scrimmage. Now a man, now a horse, fell to the ground but was on his feet again in a twinkling. I had never seen a more wonderful exhibition of skilled riding. The sheep was torn into a thousand pieces and when a horseman freed himself from the scrum and rode towards us to lay his booty at the Khan's feet a dozen others followed in hot pursuit, to snatch his booty from him at the last moment, and we had frequently to take to flight ourselves so as not to be ridden down in the excitement of the chase.

When the game had lasted about an hour the Khan called a halt. Not less than four dozen horsemen dashed up, laughing and shouting, each with a bleeding piece of sheep in his hands.

Then came the awarding of the prizes. An old greybeard, sitting on his horse held a large balance and weighed all the gory fragments in turn. The prizes were distributed strictly according to weight. Horses, bridles, fur caps, carpets, and my ten tumans were handed over to the lucky winners. The amazing thing was that with all the wild riding and falling not a single man or horse was hurt. A mighty feast concluded the show.

That evening the Khan and his two sons visited me in my yurt. I begged Alim Qul to tell me something about his own life and the history of the Turkomans.

His original name had been Muhammad Qul. While the fighting round Gök Tapa was in progress the Yomut had heard that Alim Qul, the heroic Khan of Khoqand, had fallen at Tashkent in battle against the Russians. They immediately transferred the name of the hero of Turkistan to their own young chieftain, Muhammad Qul,

Drinking tea, loafing, and telling stories are the main occupations of the Turkoman menfolk – when not raiding

that the Russians might believe that their most dreaded enemy had come to life again.

The original home of the Turkomans was the Mangishlaq peninsula on the Caspian. They are now divided into several tribes: the Ersari live on the left bank of the Amu Darya (Oxus) and extend deep into Afghanistan; the Sakar inhabit the deserts and oases between Merv and Andkhui; the Sariq are found in the Panj Deh and Kushk on the Afghan border; the Salor upstream on the Murghab River; the Tekke are at home in the mountains of Kuren Dagh and the oasis of Merv; the Yomut travel through the deserts east of the Caspian and far up into the Khanate of Khiwa, while some of the Chaudor have remained in the Mangishlaq peninsula and others of them have settled in the north of Khiwa. The total number of Turkomans, reckoning all the tribes together, was at that time round about 1,000,000 souls. Their sturdy independence and unconquerable passion for freedom was tending to drive them more and more into those regions over which the Russians were able to exercise only imperfect control. The fact that the Russians had declared their country an autonomous republic in alliance with the Soviet Union had done nothing to alter their feelings. Their highest law, the Dab, is tradition and custom. They never deviate from it by a hair's breadth, so that the Turkoman of today lives exactly as his forefathers of a thousand years ago. If any one attempts to abrogate one of their laws or customs, or if the Russians seek to bring them in the very slightest degree under state supervision, they simply strike their tents and wander off to other places in the immeasurable wastes of the Black Sand, the Qara Qum, into which very few Europeans have as yet ventured.

Their religion is that of the Sunni Muhammadans, but they are not unduly puritanical and interpret the Quran with considerable freedom. They show not the slightest consideration towards their women, who are treated as slaves and expected to attend to all agricultural as well as all domestic work. The men hunt, get up displays and jousts on horseback, or indulge in raiding; otherwise they live a leisured life of uninterrupted ease. Few Turkomans live in permanent settlements. They are either nomads or semi-nomads, who use their more permanent headquarters only in winter. The most stationary are the Yomut and the Tekke, whose women make the most beautiful carpets and the richest in colouring that are found in the East. At the same time the Yomut and the Tekke are the poorest of the tribes. Their poverty is at the bottom of the notorious lust for plunder which to this day makes them greatly dreaded. This accounts also for their passion for fine horses, whose speed contributes to the success of their attacks on caravans and towns. Second only to his love of hospitality is the Turkoman's love of his horse. He may live in rags himself; his horse will be covered with costly saddlecloths, while its harness and saddle gleam bright with silver platings. The favourite horse is usually housed in the family yurt.

Alim Qul displayed not the slightest reserve in recounting robber raids which he had organised and in the most of which he had himself taken part. In such excursions the Turkomans are out not only for the cattle and movables of their victims but also for prisoners. If these cannot raise a ransom they are kept as slaves.

In their raids the Turkomans spare only fellow Sunnis and Jews. The latter are considered unclean, and the former are respected as co-religionists whom it is not seemly to enslave. Alim Qul boasted that under his rule in Gök Tapa he had captured altogether some 70,000 Persian Shiahs, whom they had sold as slaves. He saw nothing in this worthy of comment, still less anything reprehensible.

Fights against the invading Russians had begun in 1880. Four years later General Skobeleff invested Alim Qul's fort of Gök Tapa. Not less than 26,000 well-armed Russians were opposed to approximately 8,000 Yomut and Tekke under the command of my host. The Russians had thirty-six pieces of artillery, with which they bombarded the primitive towers and walls. With incredible courage the Turkomans undertook a sortie, cut down a lot of Russians, captured two cannons, and brought them with numerous prisoners back into their fort. The natives had no idea how to work

31

the guns and tried to compel the Russian prisoners to load and fire them. Alim Qul narrated with admiration how one Russian had behaved when the Turkomans sought to force him to use the guns against his fellow countrymen. Even after they had hacked off his toes and fingers one by one, he still refused. Finally they flayed him alive and he died in agony.

I stayed for a fortnight in the *aul* with my Turkoman friends and learned to know the people better than many a Russian does in a lifetime. I was sorry to quit this lonely desert village, but I had decided to push on to Aidin (not to be confused with the town of the same name in Asia Minor), and then to travel by rail to Qizil Arwat to see Steinschneider.

The entire population of the *aul* accompanied us far out into the desert, as I rode away with Khores and Shir Dil. We proposed to ride by Gamajiki and Ana Qurban to the *aul* Arsan Qaya, where Shir Dil was to take his leave of us and return home, while Khores insisted on coming with me all the way to Qizil Arwat.

On the seventh day of our desert journey we came to the river Uzboi, which, at several points on its way to the Caspian, vanishes completely into the sands of the desert, to reappear ten or twelve miles farther on. We followed the course of the Uzboi for a spell and then branched off towards the east. Eight days after leaving our *aul* we struck the railway, and two hours later saw ahead the houses of Aidin. Shir Dil now said farewell and repeatedly begged me to visit him again on my return journey.

III

Into the Forbidden Land

A train journey of just under a hundred miles brought us to Qizil Arwat. I lay low in a tea-house in the bazaar while Khores went off to find Steinschneider. They soon appeared together. I had not seen my old friend since 1919, five years before. He had in the meantime become completely acclimatised and was so much the Russian that I scarcely recognised him. I explained my plan to him in German. I wanted the loan of his identification papers and with these I would present myself to the Agricultural and Mineralogical Department in Ashqabad or Qaghan as a geologist who wished to investigate the mineral resources of the mountains of Bukhara and the possible sites of ore and coal mines. If my scheme was approved I should be free to travel to and fro through the country at will without attracting attention or being held up. If the authorities would not accept my services in this capacity, I should simply have to think out some other plausible pretext. I was quite clear that it would be unwise to proceed to the city of Bukhara unless I had express permission to do so.

Steinschneider thought my plan an admirable one and would dearly have liked to accompany me. He was only deterred by the reflection that I should then have no papers and that duplicate Steinschneiders would be apt to excite comment. We agreed that in any unforeseen contingency he would say that his papers had got lost; and that in no circumstances would he admit that he had ever seen or known me. I promised to return, if possible, by way of Qizil Arwat and restore his documents with my own hand. We then bade each other good-bye.

33

Khores then set out to try to change my Persian tumans for chervonitz,[1] a business which he thought he could negotiate amongst his Turkoman friends. This proceeding was fraught with some danger, for technically only the branches of the State Bank and the co-operative societies under them had the right to deal in currency. Here in Central Asia the bank officials would inevitably ask a European very awkward questions about the source of his foreign money – a thing which I naturally wanted to avoid. In a few hours Khores returned and handed me over a bundle of greasy rouble notes, for gold chervonitz were not to be had. He came back from the bazaar with a piece of news which surprised as much as it delighted me. He had decided to come with me himself and pay a visit to his brother-in-law in Hazrat Bashir. I was only too glad to accept this offer.

That very evening I took two tickets, and Khores and I mounted the train bound for Charjui some five hundred miles away, the then capital of the Turkmenistan Soviet Republic. The incredible cheapness of travel on the Russian railways took my breath away. For a journey rather longer than from Vienna to Lake Constance I paid 31 roubles apiece, say about £2 19s., for our seats in an express train. This sum gave us a right to a sleeping-place and indefinite supplies of boiling water for tea. Trusting to Stein-schneider's identification papers I decided to break the journey at Ashqabad. This town had for some time been known as Poltoratsk, but it had been re-altered to the original name of Ashqabad after the fighting of 1920.

This oasis had been the headquarters of the fighting which for a whole year had raged through southern Turkistan, bringing devastation in its train. The English general, Malleson, coming by forced marches from Persia, brought some Indian regiments and a few British regulars to the assistance of the anti-revolutionaries. Instead of joining them immediately, Malleson first struck westwards with his troops, crossed the Caspian, and occupied the oil wells of Baku,

1   See note, p. 222.

for the moment supplying the rebels only with provisions, arms, and ammunition.

The Government of Tashkent, under the illusion that they had to deal only with a small local insurrection of a few wealthy Turkoman khans, instructed some Soviet commissars under the command of the redoubtable Poltoratsk to proceed to Ashqabad, arrest the khans and put the trouble down in a few days. Some delegates of the Turkoman tribes and of the local Russian population presented themselves, unarmed, on the platform to treat with the Government emissaries. Poltoratsk announced that he would have no dealings with rebels and counter-revolutionaries. The Ashqabad delegates retorted that in that case they would not permit the commissars to set foot in the town. Hereupon Poltoratsk flung a hand-grenade into the unarmed assembly, killing sixteen. Half an hour later the train was surrounded and the commissars were slain along with their military escort.

In the long run Poltoratsk's impetuous gesture cost the lives of 64,000 people. When autonomy was granted to Turkmenistan the first act of the Government of the new republic was to wipe the hated name of Poltoratsk off the map and restore to Ashqabad its original title.

Ashqabad, with some 80,000 inhabitants, is today the second largest town in Turkmenistan and is renowned for its Turkoman carpets and for its sweet melons. In the centre of the oasis rise the lofty mud walls of the fort, which commands a view of the entire city. Near it is the palace of the Turkoman khan, Shir Ali, now in ruins, but once famous for the wonderful mosaics with which it was adorned. After a two-day halt in the Hôtel Swerdloff – which might have been an elder brother of the Hôtel Paris in Enzeli, for it was if possible even dirtier and more tumbledown – we continued our journey eastwards. Most of the qishlaqs, or villages, which lay in the oasis near the railway line were now represented solely by heaps of mud, for the Turkomans who had inhabited them had defended themselves to the last man and their houses had been blown to pieces. At Lutfabad the railway approaches within a few miles of the Persian border, which is formed by the steep rocky cliffs of the outliers of the Küpat Dagh and Ala Dagh ranges and the Kuh i Mirabi. Every now and then you can see at one and the same time, planted on the mountains, the flag of the Soviets with its star and the Persian flag with its lion. After Dushaq the train crosses about 330 miles of the Qara Qum, the Desert of Black Sand, which name, however, is a misnomer, for the colour of the sand varies from light yellow to greyish brown. There are only two oases in this long stretch.

After a run of five hours the train drew up in the oasis of Merv, which, like the oasis of Tejen, is amply provided with water from the numerous branches of a river. The Murghab rises in the Band i Turkistan Mountains of Afghanistan, is joined at Panj Deh by the small tributary of the Kushk, and after passing through Merv loses itself, like the Tejen (the lower course of the Hari Rud), in the wildernesses of the Qara Qum.

It was from Merv that I had started my flight out of Turkistan, in 1916, which was to lead me through a sector of northern Afghanistan and through the whole of Persia. My feelings were deeply stirred as I saw the station again and thought of the contrast between then and now. Then, I was flying out of the country by stealth; now, I had entered it again, no less by stealth. While I stood there sunk in thought, a Turkoman gendarme suddenly accosted me and demanded my identification papers. This was the first time since I had set foot in Turkistan on the banks of the Atrak that any one had asked to see my papers; now I was to test whether my friend's documents would pass muster. Not without some quickening of the pulse I drew them out and handed them to him. He examined them with care, thanked me, and handed them back; and the stone that metaphorically rolled from my heart was assuredly as big as the mountain massif of Paropamisus which gleamed rosy red across the frontier of Afghanistan.

The oasis of Merv is entirely surrounded by the waterless Qara Qum, and thus for centuries remained impregnable. Though the robber raids of the Turkomans frequently called for the vengeance of Persians, Afghans, Bukharans, and Khiwans it was seldom that a hostile army succeeded in penetrating to Merv. The sand of the desert served the Turkomans better than any fortification.

The first brush between Russians and Turkomans occurred in 1859 on the east coast of the Caspian Sea. The Russians were again and again repulsed and the fight for Merv lasted a good quarter of a century, till the Russians at last gained possession of it in 1884.

I was anxious to explore some part of the Qara Qum while I was in Merv and to achieve this ambition I joined a caravan that was setting out for Khiwa. I proposed to ride with it as far as the wells of Qoyun Quyu, and wait there for a caravan coming in the opposite direction, with which I should return to Merv.

We left Merv in the early morning. Slowly and with dignified circumspection the camels planted their feet in the muddy morass formed by the seepage of the river, which floods the whole country in autumn and spring, and makes it one of the worst malaria-breeding places in Turkistan. The camel bells tinkled in the thin air of morning and made that magic music which is inseparable from the very thought of a caravan.

After we left the marshes the sand dunes began, at first occasionally broken by the yellow-green grass of the steppes. As we advanced farther and farther from water the grass disappeared completely. The sand glittered in the sun as if it were composed of microscopic spangles. The spangles are in reality minute salt crystals, which are often so numerous that the landscape recalls the salt tracts of Persia.

Our course lay along one of the oldest caravan routes of Central Asia, by which the armies of Alexander had travelled from Khiwa southwards on their all-defying march to India. Our first halt was in the middle of the desert. The bales of goods which formed the camel-loads were in a trice built up into walls to protect us from the wind. We had brought firewood along with us and soon camp fires were flickering on all sides, and basins of green Indian tea were circulating, while the *chilim* passed from mouth to mouth. The leader of the caravan, who had been trekking across the desert, winter and summer, for eight and twenty years, told us of his experiences, and while he was still describing his battles with desert robbers one fire after another went out. We rolled ourselves in our bedding and soon the only sound to be heard was the grumbling of a few restless camels.

I lay long awake staring into the cloudless sky, lit by the brilliance of uncounted stars. From the middle of April till the end of October the sky of Turkistan is pure and clear. Not a drop of rain, not a cloud, is seen during these six months, so that every journey or excursion can be planned six months ahead, without a fear that the weather will play false. Old, experienced travellers like my caravan companions make an art of unloading their camels quickly in the evening and loading up with equally magic speed for the morning's march. When the leader, Yulji Cholbaieff, woke me at sunrise the animals were already saddled and loaded. I hastily drank my tea, munched a few raisins with it – our only substitute for sugar – and rolled up my felt blanket. Then I settled myself in the saddle of my riding camel, and the animal's motion soon lulled me again to sleep. I would wake with a start every now and then, just as I was on the point of falling off.

We reached the well of Shaikh Mansur, where we pitched our second desert camp. I was awakened in the morning by the trampling of many camels, and jumped up in alarm, thinking our caravan was already on the march and I had been forgotten. A Qirghiz caravan had just arrived at the well on its way to Ashqabad. It had been already thirty-six hours on the march and was short of water. In great excitement the exhausted beasts were crowding round the well.

The Qirghiz decided to halt by the water till next day, and set about unloading and unsaddling their pack camels and horses. Just beside me a horseman lifted the shapeless saddle off his pony and when he took off the felt blanket that had been underneath I was shocked at the ghastly bleeding flesh that was revealed. I was just going to reproach the man bitterly for letting his horse get into such condition when I realised that what I had taken for wounds were in fact thin strips of raw meat which the rider had put under the saddle to prevent chafing. When I inquired about the matter I learned that the Qirghiz and Tartars are in the habit of thus protecting the places where the pressure of the saddle comes, and that by this means an incipient wound is cured before it develops. My horseman had been unable for a long time to unsaddle his pony, so he had shot a gazelle as he came along and laid the fresh flesh on the pony's back under the saddle. It is this practice, perhaps, which has given rise to our school-book legend that the invading Huns who came from Asia used to ride on their fresh-killed meat to make it tender.

IV

Across the Qara Qum to Samarqand

The rest of our journey to the well of Qoyun Quyu was extremely heavy going, for this part of the desert consists of sand dunes ninety feet high and more, the ascent and descent of which is most laborious for camels. Their long legs sink almost to the knee in the fine sand. I dismounted to make things easier for my camel by relieving him of my weight, but I soon gave up the attempt to plunge along through the burning sand, for I should have infallibly got left behind and should soon have perished of thirst if my disappearance had not been noticed.

I was hardly well in the saddle again before I saw a long cloud of dust and sand slowly approaching us from a considerable distance. I was soon able to distinguish details. There were about a hundred camels, every second one carrying a rider on its back. Unladen camels were such a rarity that I asked the caravan-*bashi*, who was ahead of me, whether these could be the celebrated desert highwaymen. I was already rejoicing in anticipation of an exciting adventure. The riders proved, however, to be the exact reverse of what I had supposed; they were a detachment of the camel corps of Desert Police and they presently drew up alongside us.

While they cross-questioned our leader about our whence and whither and examined his papers, I had a chance to study them. They were one and all young men of magnificent physique and keen features, dressed in light, pale-brown khaki, their flat, plate-like caps, with the Soviet star in front, jauntily pushed back from their forehead. All of them, including the commandant, were of the Sariq tribe of Turkomans, a race renowned in Turkistan for its

40

good looks. Mauser rifles, heavy pistols, and long-handled hand-grenades dangling from the belt, seemed to be the usual equipment amongst them. Some of the riderless camels were carrying light machine-guns, while the others were laden with water skins and tents.

The commandant of the Desert Police cross-examines our caravan leader about our purpose and destination

I got into conversation with some of the police and promised that I would send them to Charjui a few of the photographs which I had taken. This won their hearts at once, and they invited me to join their party for the rest of my journey. They were making for Yantaqli spring, and thence for Qabaqli on the lower Amu Darya. I had time enough to spare, and such an excellent opportunity of travelling safely would be unlikely to recur. I therefore accepted their invitation with alacrity. The only difficulty that presented itself was the question of mounts for Khores and myself. But the Sariq police solved it by offering us two of their reserve camels.

I paid the caravan-*bashi* the hire of the two camels we had been riding, we packed our scanty kit on to the new camels, and after cordial and oft-repeated 'Insha' Allah's' we bade farewell to our previous companions, who quickly faded into the desert.

The riding animals of the Desert Police were carefully chosen. Never, before or after, have I ridden so amenable a camel as that which now was lent to me, or one whose pace was so smooth or foot so sure. For the first half-hour I was conscious of a disturbing feeling of unrest for which I could not account. Only later did it occur to me that the police camels carried no bells. The melodious tinkling haunted my ears so persistently that at first the deprivation was definitely painful. The police naturally ride without bells, for they have no desire to advertise their coming before they are in sight, and the wind carries the sound of bells to immense distances in the thin desert air.

There was only one person who was dissatisfied with the alteration in my plans. This was Khores, who had the most profound contempt for the Sariq as tools and hangers-on of the hated Soviets and Russians. As soon as we could talk to each other without risk of being overheard he reproached me bitterly, and only my assurance that we should part from our Sariq in six days at most calmed him a little and restored his normal good temper.

Sahiyaieff, the commandant of the detachment, assured me that so far as he knew I was the only European who had ever crossed this part of the desert. The tracts between Khiwa and Merv, on the one hand, and between Khiwa and Krasnovodsk on the other, had frequently been covered by Europeans, but never the eastern section of the Qara Qum which we were now traversing.

Sand, and again sand, and nothing but sand as far as the eye could see. We proceeded at a good pace, but not until we neared the well of Qoyun Quyu did a few isolated saksaul-trees appear. We were suddenly surprised by a herd of gazelle, which dashed immediately across our path. Before I could get my rifle to the ready several shots resounded and two gazelles crashed to the ground.

They furnished us with a magnificent supper. The nearer we

drew to the well the thicker became the yellow desert grass growing between the sandhills that stretched away to the far horizon.

Next morning we quitted the caravan route we had hitherto been following, and bent our course north-west. The desert was if possible even more inhospitable in this direction. The sand was deep and fine, the unfortunate camels sank deep at every step, and we made but slow progress. The heat was murderous, the drinking water we carried was practically boiling and strongly salt, and I could not master my terrible thirst. I admired Khores and the Sariq, who never touched a drop of water the livelong day. When I complained of thirst one of the police gave me a pebble, of which he had several in his pocket. As soon as I felt it in my mouth my thirst diminished and became tolerable. My new travelling-companions told me that there were some places on the lower Amu Darya where there are piles of flattish pebbles of a convenient size and shape for carrying in the mouth. No caravan which crosses the river passes these spots without laying in a stock of them, partly to replenish their own store and partly to serve as presents to other caravans whose course does not take them to the river and who are grateful for the gift.

Towards evening a light wind arose, carrying a lot of sand with it and making riding a perfect torment, for in a second eyes, mouth, and nose were choked with it. It grew stronger and stronger and the blown grains of sand larger and larger. We were riding into a regular *buran*, such as I had encountered nine years ago in Üch Aji. In such weather there was not the slightest hope of making Yandaqli that day, so the soldiers decided to pitch camp early for the night. The saddles were hastily snatched off and built up into a screen from the wind. The storm was by now raging so fiercely that cooking was not to be thought of, so we rolled ourselves in our felt blankets and huddled under the couched camels for protection. When I woke, the storm was still raging and my blankets were crushing me under an intolerable weight. I endeavoured to get free and rolled over till the blanket opened. When I crept out of it, I saw that the sleeper beside me was buried under a layer of sand nearly four inches thick. So that was the weight that had been oppressing me; I shook my blanket free of sand and quickly crept into it again under the shelter of my camel.

Not till ten o'clock next forenoon did the *buran* abate. One after another we shook ourselves out of the sand, and fires were soon ablaze. The huge tea kettles were put on and we gratefully swallowed the hot drink. In spite of every effort to get clean, it was not till I was able to get a bath in the Amu eight days later that I finally felt my body completely free from sand. I cannot conceive how the Qirghiz manage with their horses and donkeys in such a storm. The camels are masters of the art of crouching in such a way that their heads are as far as possible protected from the driving sand. But horses and donkeys have no such skill, and they are terrified by the driving sand. I asked Sahiyaieff about this, but he had no idea what the Qirghiz did, for he had never been with one of their caravans in a sandstorm.

That afternoon we at last reached the well. Its waters were, however, so thick with sand and so salt that we could only water the camels, but had ourselves to refrain from drinking. We had been looking forward eagerly to the taste of fresh water, for the water we had with us in sheepskins was already eight days old and had been all the time exposed to the direct rays of the burning sun.

To make matters worse, the skins were only crudely tanned and they imparted a strong smell to their contents, which were brackish to start with. One gulp of this liquid was enough to make one feel deadly sick. These considerations decided Sahiyaieff to give up his original destination of Qabaqli on the Amu in the north-east of the Qara Qum; for he was afraid that the sand-storm would have made all the springs on the route undrinkable. He therefore swerved east and made for Iljik, in the hopes of reaching fresh water sooner. Though both we and the camels were in sore need of a longer rest, we pushed on at once. By night the temperature was somewhat less intolerable and thirst eased off a little. I crouched on my camel, tired and dead to the world, and every now and then dozed a few minutes as I rode. Even when the ball of the sun rose burning red over the edge of the waste, Sahiyaieff would not allow a halt. We had ridden all through the night with only an hour's halt during which we had made the last of our drinking water into tea. If we could not reach the Amu before sunset we should perish to a man.

That day was the most terrible that I have ever lived through. Palate and tongue were so utterly dried up and saliva so entirely non-existent that even the faithful pebble in my mouth could not coax forth the tiniest drop of moisture. After some hours everything suddenly went black before my eyes and I began to rock helplessly to and fro in the saddle. I tried to hold tight and steady myself, but crashed to the ground and knew no more.

When I came to, I found myself drenched from head to foot and heard the voices of many men round me. I opened my eyes and saw Khores and a lot of Qirghiz standing round. A few yards from my bed of reeds a huge river was rolling its mud-yellow flood towards the north. I was lying on the banks of the Amu Darya, to which the Sariq had carried me. They themselves had started off again long since, and were well on their way downstream towards Qabaqli.

For four days I lay in the reed-tents of the Qirghiz, accumulated a mass of lice, and caught a full-size attack of malaria, which declared itself a few days after. Qannadi would have greeted my conduct with benevolent comment, for I drank gallons of the river water without boiling it. I simply could not swallow enough of the muddy mixture, so incomparably sweet it tasted – water free of salt. While I had been lying unconscious the Qirghiz had got their magician medicine-man to treat me. He poured water over me again and again, leaped round me to drive out the evil spirits from my body, and beat his magic drum the while with incomparable perseverance.

On the fifth day the steamer called at last, took us on board, and brought us upstream to Charjui. On the way we watched Russian fishermen hauling their catch ashore. Khores somewhat cynically remarked that we could have reached the same goal considerably more cheaply and with less fatigue if we had taken the train from

Merv! Our old tub made but slow headway against the current, less because of the speed of the river than the strong resistance offered by the sand with which it was laden. At Deinau on the left bank we were unable to draw in to shore, so much sand had piled up against the bank. Some Qirghiz passengers who wished to land had to be sent ashore in boats. We did not reach Khoja Qala till next day, after circumnavigating several islands in the river. This is the first Bukharan frontier fortress on this stretch of the Amu Darya. The river is about a mile and a quarter across at this point, but widens further before Charjui to about two and a quarter. To avoid the dangers of floods, Khoja Qala is built a mile or so inland on the top of a hill, and numerous canals from the Amu irrigate the land round the fort, which boasts a population of about a hundred.

On account of the moving sandbanks the captain resolutely refused to stir at night, and we cast anchor opposite the fortress. Our steamer got under way again at daybreak. The river flows through dreary barren desert, and past many fortress-like but ruined buildings which the people of Bukhara built in former days as a defence against the Turkomans. Towards midday we saw the first cultivation, and in the late afternoon we tied up at the narrowest part of the river, not far from the steel bridge of Charjui, which is well over a mile long.

Charjui itself lies over three miles from the river. I at once announced myself to the river customs officer on the bank and begged him to order me a cart for the drive to the town. First he asked to see my *bumaga*, or papers, which I produced without misgiving after my reassuring experience of their acceptability in Merv. But this almighty man declared that they were not sufficient; I needed a permit from the Soviet of Charjui before he could allow me to land. He would not understand that I had come to Charjui expressly in order to get one. When, however, I expressed my willingness to leave Khores and my baggage in his charge, he consented to let me ride to the town, and even lent me his own horse for the purpose.

46

V

In the Lion's Den

The Soviet had set up its offices in the house of the wealthy tea-merchant Arghamanoff, who had been killed in the rising of 1919. A huge red flag at the entrance and a notice which in five languages – one of which was German – summoned the proletarians of all countries to unite, immediately proclaimed the house to be the seat of a Government department.

It was by no means an easy task to secure admission to the presence of the Chief Commissar, Comrade Uranyaiff. The dignified officials, who were almost without exception Turkomans, could not understand what a European who wore neither uniform nor revolver could possibly want with the chief. Not until I hit on the expedient of whispering mysteriously into their ears that my business was highly confidential, not to say 'secret', could I induce them to send my name in to the omnipotent one.

He was drinking tea and smoking a hubble-bubble when I came in. He received me and pointed to a chair. I sat down without further ceremony, and the following is the gist of what I told him: 'Comrade Uranyaiff! In the mountains of the frontier districts of Turkmenistan there are unquestionably large quantities of undiscovered treasure. I do not mean treasure such as the bourgeois capitalists of former times might have buried there; I mean metal ore, coal, or salt. I am a geologist by profession and I have hitherto been working in the Soviet interests in Qizil Arwat. But I have come to think that I can be of more use to the Soviets if I use my expert knowledge to locate these treasures and help to make them available for use. I can of course only hope to do this if you will

47

entrust me with full powers to travel freely through the districts where I suspect these riches to be concealed. If you will supply me with the necessary documents, riding animals, and technical equipment, I am prepared to work in the sole interests of the Soviet of Turkmenistan and to reveal to you all the mines or deposits I may discover, without asking any reward for myself.'

'Tovarish Steinschneider, I am delighted that you are willing to undertake the labour of this task. But I cannot come to a decision on my own responsibility alone. I shall call a committee and give you an answer in the course of the next week.'

'Tovarish Uranyaiff, that is extremely kind of you. But the customs officer on the river was unwilling even to let me enter your town, and would not accept as valid the identification papers which I hold from the Town Soviet of Qizil Arwat. I must beg you therefore to grant me an authorisation to remain here while I await your reply.'

'That priceless idiot of a customs officer! Of course you shall have the necessary *bumaga* at once. Just excuse me a few moments.'

I breathed again. Everything was working out according to plan. After the wait of what really *was* only a few moments I had the permit for Khores and myself safely in my pocket. I hastened off to the nearest inn to get myself something hot to eat. I found a decent eating-house near the railway station and at the door of it a man selling newspapers. I bought myself the latest number of the Russian *Ashqabad News*, went in and ordered some skewers of grilled *shishlik*. Meantime I started to read the paper – and nearly dropped it in dismay. I read that in Qizil Arwat, Shock-worker Steinschneider had been struck by a broken transmission belt and seriously injured.

Russian newspapers usually deal only in politics and economics, but shock-workers hold in industry the position as it were of officers in the army and their pictures are reproduced in the local newspapers much as film stars are with us, so a full account of my friend's accident was given.

I left my *shishlik* untasted, leaped into the saddle, and rode hell for leather towards the banks of the Amu. There I showed the river customs officer my *bumaga*, procured the cart I wanted, and drove with my kit straight to the station. Off out of Charjui before it was too late! Khores couldn't make out what had happened, but I urged him to keep as far away as possible from me, so that if I were arrested he should not be mixed up in the business. As, however, he absolutely refused to budge from my side, I bade him stay by my kit and watch it while I went back into the town, for there were still seven hours before the train was due to start. I reminded myself that except for the customs man and the Chief Commissar not a soul in Charjui knew my name – or rather, the name I was passing under – and that in any case I was safer anywhere than in the station, which was just the place they would first look for me. My appetite, however, was clean gone!

For the first time in my life I was really afraid, and I made a note of the fact that advancing age undermines a man's courage and enterprise. It wasn't nine years since I had been arrested in this very town as an escaped prisoner of war – and the whole thing had been a lark. In that spirit I had treated the authorities and the guards who had arrested me; I had genuinely enjoyed making fun of them. This time I took matters much more seriously, and at every corner I came to I peered cautiously round to see if a gendarme was at my heels.

Charjui is the centre of Turkmenistan's cotton production, and wherever you go everything speaks of cotton. A lot of new factories had been recently built, all of them in the service of cotton. Most of them were ginning mills, where a series of circular saws, ranged alongside each other, separate the seed from the fibre. The latter is then compressed into bales and dispatched to Russia to be spun. The seeds are pressed on the spot to extract the oil, which yields the so-called 'fast-day fat'. It is coal black as it flows from the primitive presses, but when purified with caustic soda turns a golden yellow like olive oil, and is welcomed for all kinds of cooking. The refuse yields a valuable, much-prized cattle food, and is also sometimes used as fuel for heating.

Hundreds of carts and long camel caravans were bringing in the raw cotton, or carrying the bales of pressed fibre to the station or the landing stages on the river. The Soviets' second Five-Year Plan had just come into operation, and large stretches of country had been freshly planted with cotton instead of corn – a proceeding which was to avenge itself bitterly the following year, when a severe corn shortage set in.

I strolled along through the Turkoman quarter towards the bazaar and sat down in a *chai-khana*. Formerly the only decorations of a tea-house consisted of pictures cut from the illustrated papers, or the covering of a chocolate box. Now photographs of Lenin predominate, or of Khidiralieff, or of the local commissars of the autonomous republics. You meet here representatives of the most diametrically opposed philosophies mixing in perfect accord. The red flag floats over the entrance to all public buildings and little red pennons adorn every tiny booth and shop, either because the proprietor is a genuine communist or because he wishes to pose as one. So you may see a praying carpet rolled in a corner with a Quran on top of it ready for immediate use, while above these mute witnesses to Islam a red flag flutters, or the picture of a Soviet leader hangs. In Russia proper the anti-god campaign is vigorously waged by the State, and its dogmas diligently preached, but the religion of Muhammad had remained so far unassailed in the autonomous Soviet republics of Central Asia, and it will probably so remain for a long time to come, though emissaries from Moscow are doing their best to undermine it. In the newly founded schools every effort is made to influence the children against Islam.

The former fortress of the Beg now houses a museum, which mainly displays old weapons, rolls of papyrus, instruments of torture, and communist posters. The most interesting exhibit is a large collection of Turkoman musical instruments, none of which, however, have the value of rarity, for all of them are still in everyday use. One of the horns would certainly be reckoned an ornament to any west European collection. It is close on ten feet long and in appearance very similar to our Alpine horns. It is composed entirely

Niya Qurban Neppez, reputed to be the last surviving descendant of Timur

of tiny bits of camel-bone pieced together and is richly ornamented with silver bands set with turquoise. This horn is so heavy that three men have to support it on their shoulders while a fourth is blowing it. A large number of drums, not unlike our kettle-drums, up to ten of which one man can play at a time, and a handsome old *surnai* – resembling a clarinet – complete the collection.

In the fortress the visitor is shown the prison that was in use until 1920. It was only used for Bukharan subjects who were under the jurisdiction of the Beg. I crept through a tiny opening, barely half a yard square, into an underground dungeon, which naturally boasted neither window nor ventilator. By the light of a torch I saw the two side walls, about nine feet six inches long, into each of which were built in six neck and foot rings, so that a wall-space about one foot seven inches wide was allotted to each prisoner. In the centre of the cell there were two sets of stocks let into the floor, each made to take four people. The room was four feet nine inches high and I reckoned that the twenty prisoners enjoyed the total air space of about thirteen and a half cubic yards. There were seven similar cells. When the Turkomans drove out the Beg in 1920 they set free eighty-one prisoners, many of whom were unable to move without assistance, for the height of the cell prevented their standing upright, and the neck rings prevented their lying down.

Not far from the prison I saw a Turkoman woman who was wearing an exceptionally valuable breast ornament, while at work in a field of cotton. I was told that she was Niya Qurban Neppez, and was said to be the veritable last descendant of Timur.

I went back to the station and asked Khores whether he had noticed anything suspicious in my absence. He said not. I then took two tickets for Samarqand. The happy-go-lucky methods of the Soviet authorities are notorious, and I set out with an easy mind, convinced that anyhow no one in Charjui would wonder why the reputed geologist had failed to reappear.

After a journey of nearly fourteen hours, past Qaghan and Katta Qurghan, we reached the former capital of Timur and then capital of the Soviet Republic of Uzbegistan, about 232 miles distant from

Charjui. The Turkistan trains crawl incredibly slowly through the desert. The sleepers are simply laid flat in the sand, and since no renewals or repairs have been done to the permanent way since 1914 the trains are obliged to creep along the lines with the utmost caution, though these are laid as straight as a die and curves are almost non-existent.

I had left Samarqand four years ago, and never dreamt then that I should one day come back. I calmly asked a gendarme what hotel he could recommend, for since my last stay all the hotels had been nationalised and were being used as soldiers' barracks. Without asking to see my passport he recommended the Hotel Freedom in the Abramoffsky Boulevard.

Samarqand was dangerous ground for me to tread, and I had to exercise the greatest care not to be seen and recognised by any of my numerous acquaintances of former days. Some of the ex-prisoners of war had remained on here, and though I could implicitly trust their loyalty and goodwill, an incautious word from one of them might make an unwilling traitor of him. So I decided to hang about the station till after dark, and sent Khores on ahead with my baggage to the hotel. While he went off, I myself wandered to what used to be the summer headquarters of the Cossacks, and sat down in a small village tea-shop. Not till it was dark did I return to the station and hire a one-horse cart to drive to the town, a little over three miles from the railway.

A house belonging to a rich Bukharan Jew had been converted into an hotel. It was being run by an Armenian, and considering the conditions in Central Asia under the Soviet regime, it was not at all badly equipped. I liked the position of the hotel, which lay obliquely opposite the buildings of the old Russo-Asiatic Bank, now the headquarters of the Soviet Government of Uzbegistan. When I wanted to visit the authorities I should therefore not have to traipse through the town. I determined to put the credulity of the Uzbegistan officials to the test the first thing on the morrow.

In the days of the Tsars, Tashkent had been the residence of the governor, and under the new regime it had been until the previous year the capital of the whole of Turkistan. The new Soviet Constitution of 1924–5 – which was doomed, however, to be again radically changed in 1927 – had divided Turkistan into three autonomous republics: Turkmenistan, with a population of 1,174,000 and an area of approximately 174,000 square miles; Uzbegistan, with a population of 827,000 and an area of approximately 60,544 square miles; Tajikistan, with a population of 1,209,000 and an area of approximately 56,641 square miles. At the same time the much smaller town of Samarqand was made the capital of the Uzbeg Republic. Tajikistan comprises the south-eastern part of Turkistan up into the Pamir plateau, while northern Turkistan was added to the Qirghiz Republic of Qazaqistan.

This is perhaps a suitable moment to say something about the political atmosphere of Russian Central Asia at this period.

The Russian attempt to bolshevize Central Asia may justly be considered one of the most interesting political experiments in the world history of the last eighteen years. The distrust with which England has of late regarded Soviet Russia is easily explained, for Britain feels her rule in India and Baluchistan to be threatened. Under the Romanoffs the Russians were content to extend their sphere of economic influence, while the Soviets seek to attack the national and social side of Britain's overlordship in Asia. This is the Soviets' sole reason for according a certain independence and autonomy to the Asiatic races. They want to be able to point out to kindred peoples and co-religionists across the border that the Muslims whose territories belong to the U.S.S.R. are free from foreign domination. The existence of the various Russian 'advisers' of the national governments is represented as being merely temporary and incidental. The advisers are to hold office only until the Asiatic peoples of Russia are ripe for the independent administration of their own countries. The truth is naturally the exact opposite. The advisers are the real rulers, without whose concurrence not a sheet may fall to the ground from the desk of the Tsik (the Central Executive Committee); the rules for administration are issued either direct by Stalin himself or else by the Moscow Comintern (Communist International).

Their efforts to achieve political expansion in Asia were bound to bring the Bolshevists up against their natural enemy; and their natural enemy of course is England. Long before the rest of the world had realised the danger threatening in the East, the British foresaw and tried to forestall it by sending General Malleson to invade Turkistan from Persia. Operating along the Persian frontier he pushed forward to Charjui, made himself master of the Amu Darya, and seized the Central Asian Railway. The indigenes of every race and all anti-Bolshevists, more especially the tsarist officials and officers, enthusiastically supported the British and hailed them as liberators. Malleson had penetrated some seven hundred miles into the country when the Americans, French, and Italians exerted pressure on the British Government and Malleson was recalled. The Powers were afraid of a further extension of the British Empire in Asia, and were especially jealous of Britain's possession of the invaluable oil wells of Baku, which Malleson had seized immediately on his arrival in the Caucasus. The world-power, Oil, defeated Britain, and is therefore the unqualified, if unforeseen, promoter of Bolshevism in Central Asia; for the Bolsheviks, hemmed in on every front, could not possibly have ejected the British by their own unaided efforts.

The first step the Soviets took was to lay a bait for Persia. By a few skilful manoeuvres they contrived to gain enormous economic advantages for themselves and oust the British from their secure position. The cancellation of the agreements with the Anglo-Persian Oil Company was the first fruits of their success. In reward for this they made the Persians a present of fifty-three or fifty-four miles of the railway which runs from Julfa to Tabriz. The Russian statesman Troyanoffsky then published a memorandum in which he designated India a Britain's Achilles' heel and Persia as the Suez Canal of the Asiatic Revolution. Turkey's ex-Minister for War, Enver Pasha, who had fled into exile, played in these proceedings a considerable role, which I shall mention in a moment.

Conditions in Afghanistan were equally propitious for Russia's intrigues. The anti-Bolshevist Amir, Habib Ullah, had been murdered in 1919. He was succeeded by Aman Ullah, who was reputed a free-thinker and a friend of Europe. Under his influence the Soviets were able to strengthen their position enormously, while a definite anti-British policy held the field until the summer of 1919.

Between Afghanistan, destined to be the victim of Russian expansionist policy, and Russian Turkistan there lay the buffer state of Bukhara. As soon as Malleson had been withdrawn from Turkistan the Russians had an easy task to re-establish their rule. When peace had been restored they allowed themselves a breathing space and assembled a large number of Red troops on the borders of Bukhara, chiefly in the neighbourhood of the capital. One fine day the artillery of the Red Army opened fire on the city, while at the same moment numerous detachments marched into the country at various points and quickly suppressed the feeble resistance offered them. The Amir of Bukhara fled to Afghanistan and committed the task of reconquering his country to Enver Pasha, who, though he had been sent out by Lenin, was determined to pursue separatist ideals of his own. Enver Pasha was suspected by the Cheka, hunted down, and duly 'liquidated', in the favourite Russian phrase!

In my later journeys through east Bukhara I was successful in clearing up the many legends that had gathered round his story, and ascertaining the truth as to his fate.

In Deh i Nau, where Enver fought his last battle against the Red Army, not far from the scene of his ultimate murder, I spoke not only with people who had been eye- and ear-witnesses of his death, but with the murderer himself, who acknowledged his deed with pride as a national and patriotic act.

VI

Thus Died Enver Pasha

O n the 9th of July 1925 I met the Cheka officer Agabekoff in Deh i Nau. He had previously been a member of the Tashkent G.P.U., as the Cheka was formerly called. In the *chai-khana* at Deh i Nau I heard the truth about Enver Pasha's death. Agabekoff knew more about it than anybody else, for he had murdered him himself.

Enver Pasha was born on the 3rd of September 1882, as the son of a junior officer,[1] and went into the army as a subaltern. He was an enthusiastic Young Turk, and consequently an enemy of the then existing government. He was only twenty-six when he organised the mutiny at Salonica, and he played a distinguished part in the war in Tripoli. In the Balkan War of 1912 and 1913 he had already attained a position on the General Staff of the Turkish Army, and at the beginning of the World War, though only thirty-one, he became the all-powerful Minister for War. At the end of 1918 he was arrested and degraded. He succeeded in making his escape to Russia at the beginning of 1919, and in his absence Turkey condemned him to death.

On the 12th of February 1920 Lenin received him and sent him as his representative to the Congress of Oriental Peoples at Baku. He was there given a stirring welcome and at the end of a five-hour speech he found himself the recognised hero and leader of all freedom-seeking Muslims, representing races and tribes from the

---

1 According to another account his father was a bridge-keeper, and his mother, who was an Albanian, followed the despised profession of laying out the dead. – E.O.L.

Sir Darya to the Ganges. From Baku he travelled by Krasnovodsk to Tejen, and after many weeks of fighting put down the anti-Soviet insurrection there. Such a trifle as this did not satisfy the soaring ambition of an Enver. He dreamt of greater things, and he succeeded in convincing Lenin that it was necessary to unite the mutually-warring races of Central Asia and with their assistance first to conquer Afghanistan and then to invade India and stir up a revolution against Britain.

The two men, however, cherished incompatible ideals. Lenin saw in the united uprising of the peoples of the East the prelude to a world revolution, whereas Enver's dreams were separatist and personal. He sought nothing more nor less than to see the whole of Islam, including of course Turkey, united under his banner.

On his return from Baku he was attacked at Nikolayeffsky Ploshad by a tsarist fanatic and severely wounded, which for a time put an end to his activities. In November 1921 he roused himself again and went to Bukhara, where everything was in a state of chaos. The people welcomed him with enthusiasm. The women even tore the veils from their faces as a sign of veneration. There were at that time in Bukhara a large number of Turkish officers of pre- and post-war days, all of whom were adherents of Enver. He intended with their help to form the nucleus of a national army and restore the once mighty kingdom of Bukhara to her former greatness. These plans of his must be regarded as psychologically inevitable.

Things now began to happen with bewildering speed. Under the pretext of a hunting expedition to the former Amir's castle in Shirabad, Enver and his friends quitted Bukhara, to return a few days later at the head of a rebel army of 6,000 men. They besieged Bukhara and gave battle to the Red Army. Each side left 5,000 casualties on the field. Enver burnt down the quarter of the city round the Quyuq Mazar Gate, as well as all the country houses in the neighbourhood. After which he withdrew into the inaccessible ravines of the east Bukharan mountains.

Meantime he had got into touch with the Amir of Bukhara, who was a fugitive in Afghanistan, and offered to act as his commander-in-chief against the Soviets. This was only a ruse. Enver knew that the Amir had contrived to carry off with him in his flight his entire treasure in gold and jewels to the value of several million pounds. The nobility of Bukhara who, accompanied by their soldiers and retainers, had fled with the Amir, had a sum with them not greatly less in value. Enver wanted money to wage war and he meant to get it from the ex-rulers of Bukhara. When the right moment had come he would throw them over and realise his own designs.

The Amir appointed Enver commander-in-chief of the rebels. He had no accurate information about their numbers or their headquarters, for insurrectionary groups were scattered over the whole country and far into Turkistan. He left his new generalissimo to make all necessary inquiries and to organise the army.

The Amir's former favourite, now the Basmach Ibrahim Beg, who was 'operating' between Samarqand and Qarshi, and whose forces consisted of about 3,000 tsarist officers, Sarts, Uzbegs, and Turkomans, was at the same time put under Enver's orders. Enver was perfectly aware that he could not hope to achieve a victory over the Red Army with only these unorganised robber bands and the remnants of the original Bukharan forces. He therefore sent emissaries through the whole country, even as far afield as Khoqand, Samarqand, Khiwa, and Tashkent. He re-established the Khilafat in Turkistan and organised a general staff on the pattern of the German one, to which he had himself at one time belonged. He preached the foundation of a great Muslim state, and thus won the support of all the mullas throughout Turkistan. He offered peace to the Soviets if they would acknowledge him as the chief of the new state and give him their support. Smyrnoff, the commander-in-chief of the Red Army in Turkistan, refused the offer, and war now began in earnest. Enver recruited in Afghanistan five hundred daredevils, whom he converted into an almost invincible personal bodyguard.

His envoys did excellent work and thousands of fighting men poured in to him. He was at first successful in several actions against the Red Army and within a few weeks the whole of eastern Bukhara from the Zarafshan Mountains to Kelif on the Afghan border, was in his hands. Only in the Pamir Plateau a few scattered fragments of the Red Army still held out and embarrassed his rear, but they finally came over to him.

Intoxicated by these successes and the almost divine honours paid to his person, he disdained to heed the wishes and commands of the Amir of Bukhara. He had rashly removed the one-armed Ibrahim Beg from his command, which earned him the hate of that veteran warrior. He had a golden seal made for himself which styled him 'Commander-in-Chief of all Muslim Armies, Son-in-Law of the Khalif'.

Ibrahim Beg now stirred up the civil population, the Amir, and the army against Enver. At the same moment reinforcements reached the Russians, and the Red Army began to advance. Enver wrote to the Amir for help. The Amir sent weapons, some machine-guns, and artillery, as well as money and ammunition. The convoy was, however, betrayed by the Basmach Tughai Zarif and captured.

The mountain peoples commanded by Ibrahim Beg deserted Enver. The Russians pressed impetuously forward from the Guzar direction, while on the north Ibrahim Beg attacked at Sharshan and on the south Tughai Zarif marched against him from Shirabad. Enver had set up his headquarters in the village of Kafirnihan. Two Red Bukharan cavalry regiments surprised him there, so that he was compelled to fly for his life, abandoning almost all his food supplies and munitions. In the ravines of the Yurtchi he pitched a new camp and made sallies into the surrounding plain to collect food for the couple of thousand men who remained to him. He raided caravans belonging to the Red Army and set fire to the whole neighbourhood. The Russian command realised that there would be no peace as long as Enver was alive and at liberty. The immediate consequence was that the G.P.U. was instructed to liquidate him, and Agabekoff was selected to knife him.

I shall now let Agabekoff tell his own story:

THUS DIED ENVER PASHA

'We were ordered to capture Enver Pasha. The task was none too easy, for he shifted his ground perpetually and we had to institute a wide-flung service of spies. I decided to enter the lion's den myself disguised as a *bazaar-jik* [travelling pedlar]. In Tashkent and Bukhara I purchased a donkey and a supply of small wares. With a forged passport I succeeded in entering Qarshi, where an official of the G.P.U. was awaiting me. He was to be my liaison officer with the Red Army. On the way to eastern Bukhara I saw for the first time the devastation that the war had caused. The once flourishing countryside was a desert, broken only by the ruins of burnt villages. Some of the inhabitants had joined the Basmach, some had fled to Afghanistan or Turkistan.

'We began our business in Guzar, unpacking our wares in a *chai-khana* and getting into touch with the few folk remaining in the town. We got the Guzar merchants to give us introductions to acquaintances of theirs in Yurtchi and Deh i Nau, and these subsequently proved extremely useful. An Uzbeg of the local Soviet of Guzar was to accompany us as a guide, for he was unsuspected and had good friends everywhere. When we reached Deh i Nau we saw that the place was strongly fortified. Fighting had recently taken place in the immediate neighbourhood and when we arrived cannon and machine-gun fire was still in progress. Our friend from Guzar wandered through the neighbouring villages during the next few days and had soon spied out Enver's lair. Neither the Basmach nor the troops put any obstacle in the way of us pedlars, so we were soon able to reach the village where Enver was supposed to be staying. We settled ourselves comfortably down in a tea-house, spread out our wares, and made the acquaintance of the Basmach. By the third day we had ascertained that Enver was living in a small house standing somewhat by itself, and was vigilantly protected by his bodyguard.

'Under the pretext of needing to replenish our stocks I dispatched the G.P.U. man to the staff at Deh i Nau to say that we had tracked Enver down. The Uzbeg and I stayed on in the village. Five days later our messenger returned with the news that a cavalry

61

division had been ordered to Deh i Nau and was advancing with instructions to surround Enver and his camp.

'A couple of miles from Enver's place we met the advancing force. We gave the commandant an exact plan of the village and of Enver's house, and rode on while the detachment continued its way to complete the work we had initiated. At 7 o'clock in the morning, after having surrounded the village, the division launched the attack. The Basmach had, however, posted sentries so that the surprise missed fire. A fierce fight started but Enver's people could not stand up to our machine-gun fire and took to flight.

'Enver had sized up the situation at once and given orders to his men to hold the place till he with his staff and bodyguard had got safely away into the hills. With about fifty people he made a dash for the opposite end of the village, reached the last huts and came under the cross fire of the sixth squadron, which was posted there. A short, sharp fight ensued. Enver himself fought like a lion till he fell. The Russians drew their swords and mowed down the fugitives; only two men succeeded in escaping.

'Not a man in the division, except the commandant, had the least idea whom they were fighting. The leader, Dunoff, who had formerly served under Enver in Tejen, recognised him amongst the fallen and told his men the news. A terrific sword-stroke had cut his head clean off his body. A miniature Quran was lying by the headless corpse. Enver had obviously had it in his hand as he led his men to battle.

'The Quran was handed over to the G.P.U. in Tashkent, who added it to the file labelled "The Counter-revolutionary, Enver Pasha".'

Thus ends Agabekoff's narrative.

A few weeks later I had the opportunity of a conversation with Dunoff himself in Bukhara, and he told me that Agabekoff's story of Enver Pasha's death was a lie. According to him this was the real version of the tragedy:

'When we attacked, two riders succeeded in making their escape. One was Enver Pasha, the other was his adjutant, Zukas

Bai. They reached the spring Aqsu in the neighbourhood of the village of Arun Dar. Three men were already there resting; they were Agabekoff and his two companions. Their Turkish uniforms would have betrayed Enver and his adjutant even to the less initiated. Enver was just stooping over the sheep's skin that served as a bucket at the spring when Agabekoff whipped out the Turko-man sabre which was concealed beneath his cloak and split Enver's bent head with one blow. A second later the adjutant, completely taken by surprise, met a similar fate.'

Such was the end of the Turkish national hero, a man who had staked his life uncounted times, alike in the cause of his burning nationalism and of his insatiable personal ambition. He was barely forty, but in those few short years he had risen to incredible heights and lived through the most amazing adventures.

Enver's death rang the knell of national aspirations in Central Asia. Without him the insurrection was broken. Only a few minor leaders, like Madamin Beg, Ibrahim Beg, and Irkash Bai continued fighting on their own account. The Soviets have not succeeded even yet in checking the activity of these fanatics. Such tsarist officers as contrived to escape from Deh i Nau took flight into the mountains of the Pamirs and there joined the frontier post of the tsarist army, cut off from all communication with the outer world. Later the whole body sought refuge in China.

The Soviets bestirred themselves. Thousands of Russian propagandists flooded the country. Meantime Moscow was busy educating thousands of Muslims and training them as agitators to carry the seeds of Communism to India, Persia, and Afghanistan. The opinion in Moscow is that all difficulties in Asia will be overcome when once Bukhara, the centre of Islam, is thoroughly impregnated with the spirit of Communism. This is the key to the riddle; why does Russia keep every foreigner out of Turkistan? The races of Turkistan, passionately devoted to their century-old customs and traditions, must be preserved from any contamination by Western travellers until they are completely saturated with the dogmas of Lenin.

The morning after my arrival in Samarqand I tried to obtain an interview with Comrade Babayeff, and after circumnavigating many ugly reefs I was eventually successful. The large hall opposite the entrance, which had in former days housed the public office of the bank with its counters, etc., was now filled with writing-desks and with clerks all ostensibly buried in work. As I was talking to a Russian and trying to explain to him the object of my visit I happened to glance at a somewhat distant desk, behind which an old 'friend' of mine was working. It was Dosunyants. My heart stopped beating. This was the man who years before had de-nounced me to the Revolutionary Tribunal and had me sentenced to death.

If he had recognised me, my number was up. For the moment I turned, so as to have my back to him, and tried to get out of the unhealthy spot as soon as might be. Inwardly I cursed my folly in ever coming near Samarqand again.

At last I secured and pocketed my permit, and made my exit in such a way as not again to come into Dosunyants's range of vision. I bolted straight back to the hotel, wrote a letter to my trusty friend, the ex-prisoner of war, Kerschbaum, and bade Khores deliver it at once. I had to leave everything else to chance. In the letter I told Kerschbaum that I was back in Samarqand and that I implored him not to look me up, and to get the news round with all speed to all my former prisoner friends who might be in the town. My life depended on their not recognising me if we should happen to meet, and denying my identity if confronted with me.

Then I returned to the Soviet headquarters and sat down outside Babayeff's door till I should be granted admission. I decided to act the true and perfect Communist. When shown in I neither doffed my hat nor took the cigarette out of my mouth. With suitable variations I spun to Babayeff the same yarn as I had offered to his colleague in Charjui. The Comrade President seemed to be a man of action. He immediately summoned another comrade and ex-pounded my plans to him. Both agreed that there was a lot in my idea and it ought immediately to be followed up. The President would get the necessary documents ready for me forthwith and he asked me what equipment I should require. I asked for a cart with horse and driver, a hammer, a stone-drill, a magnifying glass, a good map of the country, two donkeys, and an order addressed to the town and village authorities to supply me with food and fodder. I then told him the route I proposed to take, and this was accepted

The central square of the Sart quarter of Samarqand, known as the Rigistan

without demur. I would travel by rail as far as Khojand, thence to Khoqand, thence across the Alai Mountains to Zanku. After Zanku I would follow the Darwaz Mountains as far as Tash Qurghan on the Chinese frontier. Thence along the Murghab (not to be confused with the other Murghab in Turkmenistan) to Qala i Wamar on the Afghan border. After this I planned to follow the line of the Ab i Panja (the Upper Oxus) to Qala i Khumb, and to continue my way by Shakh Dara, Abi Garm, Faizabad, Qurghan Tübe, Shirabad, Guzar, Qarshi, and Qasan to Bukhara, whence I hoped to return to Samarqand. All along the route I should pursue my geological researches and collect rock specimens, and on my return put all the results of my discoveries at the disposal of the Soviets. Babayeff himself suggested that in the glacier regions of the Alai and the Pamirs the cold would be extreme, and he promised therefore to issue furs and fur boots for me. He hoped to have everything ready in three days and bade me come back at the end of that time. I returned to my hotel well pleased and triumphant to find that Khores had located Kerschbaum and handed over my letter.

As soon as it was dark I ventured out again into the streets and went down the Abramoffsky Boulevard, past the church which we Austrian prisoners of war had built, and past No. 5 Barracks, where between 1915 and 1920 untold numbers of my fellow countrymen had died of starvation and typhus, leaving on my left the fortress in which Timur's throne, the Kök Tash – the Green Stone – is preserved, and crossed the wooden bridge into the Sart quarter. I hastened through the fruit and rice bazaars, where a brisk trade was still going on, towards the Shah i Zinda maze of mosques, the 'Grave of the Living King'. The moon had risen meanwhile and the numerous mosaic-covered cupolas gleamed mysteriously in her white light. I climbed a slight rise opposite the city of tombs and convinced myself that I was alone and had not been followed. Then I took out my camera and in a short time had exposed three films. I climbed over a lot of grave-mounds on my way – they look like barrels cut in half – and reached the entrance to the vaulted tombs.

I have seen many beautiful sights in various parts of the world in my time, but far the loveliest is, and will always be, the Shah i Zinda. I had visited this glorious spot at least a hundred times before, and had never ceased to long to see it once again. Shah i Zinda is the noblest and most beautiful monument of Muslim art, which even Nature shrinks from destroying. All the old buildings of Samarqand have in a greater or less degree fallen victims to the gnawing tooth of time, minarets have crumbled, vaults have tumbled in, the wonderful mosaic façades in blue and white and

The spot where Enver Pasha was murdered

green are chipping off in fragments, leaving exposed to view the yellow mud walls they used to clothe. Not so the Shah i Zinda. Cupolas and portals, walls and niches are still radiant in their marvellous blues. The open gates, adorned with lovely carving, painted with rich colour, and banded with bronze, are as well preserved as if they were of yesterday. Cupola succeeds to cupola, in each of which slumbers some long since forgotten saint.

The moon had mounted higher; her white light bathed the lonely city of the dead in magic glory. The last and loveliest of the mosques bars the path. It contains the holy well from which only the mullas are allowed to draw water. The moon was shining through the open doors and her beams reached just to the alabaster grill which covers the well. I sat down on a stone bench by the farther wall, which commanded a view back over the whole path amongst the graves. Horse-tails mounted on poles fluttered to and fro in a light breeze, casting ghostly shadows on the walls, and before I knew it I had fallen asleep.

Suddenly I woke with a start. The hasty pitter-patter of bare feet, the sound of voices and the rattle of weapons filled the air. A strange procession was passing along the track. First came a tall man, sabre in hand, his green turban and his costly robe spattered with blood, his girdle stuck full of prehistoric pistols and daggers. Even his less royally clad companions conveyed the impression of being heroes of ancient days risen from the dead. I shrank nervously back into my corner, anxious not to attract the attention of the wild performers. The mysterious figures came nearer and nearer. They halted within a few feet of me beside the holy well. A few men bent over and lifted up the heavy white alabaster covering. Their leader disappeared into the well, the men replaced the alabaster grille and ran back in the direction from which they had come. Shah i Zinda lay lonely and still in front of me when – I woke up. The impression the brief dream had made upon me was so strong that I was bathed in sweat. I made all haste to get away. As I fled down the steps I almost fell over a mulla who was sitting staring out over the graves in dignified contemplation.

The mulla hailed me and I sat down beside him, thankful to speak to a fellow being of flesh and blood. In hasty words, I told him my dream. The old man smiled. 'Allah is gracious to you,

Samarqand. The Gur i Amir, under whose dome is the tomb of Tamerlane

stranger. What you saw was no dream, but the Flight of Qasim, a cousin of Muhammad's, whose army was defeated in battle. Ever since, Qasim lives in that well, and on every anniversary he appears in the upper world. Many have seen him, but never an Unbeliever until now.'

I pressed the old man's hand and hurried towards the town. At the top of a hill I halted and cast another glance over Shah i Zinda. The cupola of the mosque in which the Muslim Barbarossa lies, blended in the moonlight with those of Ulja Ain (the nurse of Timur) and of Timur's eldest sister Jojuk Bika, forming a colour symphony in white, gold, and blue. It was perhaps the last time in my life that I should see the mausoleums of the Living King, but as long as I draw breath I shall remember their loveliness and my dream of Qasim, and shall thank my Maker that I was granted another sight of Shah i Zinda.

A great grove of tall slender poplars swallowed me up. Sunk in thought I had undesignedly found my way to the grave of Tamerlane. I looked up to the high and lofty cupola in dazzling blue, directly over which the moon had taken her stand. Was I doomed to-night not to escape from the great dead of the long vanished past? In a mud hut alongside I saw a light and knocked on the shuttered window. An aged mulla, wearing a green turban, which proclaimed the fact that he had made the pilgrimage to Mecca, stepped forth and greeted me without surprise, as if it were a matter of everyday occurrence that a stranger should come to visit Timur's grave by night.

We passed along the dark passage into the inner mausoleum. Amongst a few white gravestones stands the green slab of jade, the largest block of such nephritic crystal that the world has seen, and of simply inestimable value. A screen of marvellously carved alabaster surrounds the graves. In the corner stands a large bronze basin about the height of a man, surrounded by numerous poles carrying horse-tail banners. The great jade slab is broken in the middle. Legend tells that the dead Timur, 'turning in his grave' with wrath at the dissensions of the Faithful, sought to rise and deal forcefully with them. Even his herculean strength did not suffice to lift the slab – he only broke it. His grandson, Ulugh Beg, under whom the power of the Timurids fell into decay, engraved on his grandfather's tomb the famous words: 'Were I alive, the world would tremble.'

By the light of a torch the old mulla led me into the vaulted

A Sart girl dancing publicly in Samarqand; before 1920 she would have been stoned to death

chamber under the cupola where the actual graves of Timur's kindred are to be seen.

Face to face with the tomb of the greatest of all Asia's rulers, I asked the mulla what was the truth about Timur's being buried in Bukhara. The old man smiled indulgently: 'Timur lies here and nowhere else. The people of Bukhara proclaim that the grave of their saint Baha ud Din is Tamerlane's. That is all.'

My interest in the history of Samarqand rejoiced the old man, and he for his part questioned me about my religion. When I told him I was a Christian, he asked if he might show me the grave of Daniel (Daniel of the Den of Lions). Years before I had heard of this mysterious grave and I said I should be delighted to ride out to it that very night. We were soon mounted on two riding donkeys of the mulla's, and as they trotted off into the desert we encouraged them with guttural cries of 'Khr-khr!' We rode along past the mighty ruins of Bibi Khanum, once the greatest and costliest mosque of all Asia. We had soon left the last houses of the Sart quarter behind us and trotted in glorious moonlight across the boundless desert. The old man spoke without reserve of the mischief which Communist teaching was doing to Islam by making the new generation sceptical of their religion. Nowadays young men were rarely seen at the mosque on Friday. The number of pupils in the madrasahs was also steadily falling off, and it seemed to him that Islam was doomed to perish ere long, unless another Timur or Muqanna should arise to save it.

The time passed so quickly as we thus conversed, that I was surprised when the mulla pulled up his donkey and pointed ahead. A low sarcophagus, some nine feet six inches long, lay there in the desert sand. According to legend Daniel's body is steadily growing longer, and when it reaches a certain size he is to rise again. Behind the grave the ground fell away abruptly and in the loess cliff there was built a niche with shallow stone basins in which pious pilgrims place food for the dead saint. At the head of the grave, which is turned towards the west, there stand high poles with black horse-tails, at the foot is a bronze tablet with a Kufic inscription, while loose stones lie round about, which are displaced as Daniel grows. These roughly hewn stones enclose a rectangle of about fourteen feet by three feet six inches. Some of the stones bear primitive representations of fish, just such drawings as the followers of Jesus scratched in the sand as a sign of mutual recognition during the persecution of the Christians in Rome.

The mulla told me that Daniel grows half an inch or so every year, and every year the rectangle of stones has to be slightly enlarged. The sacred tree stands not far off, whose touch is reputed to cure leprosy. I tried to extract from my companion some more information about the cult of Daniel, but that was all that he could tell me. He himself knew nothing more. What he did know he had learned as a boy in the Ulugh Beg Madrasah and his teacher knew nothing further either. Is it possible that the legends which locate the Garden of Eden in the neighbourhood of Samarqand are something more than legends?

Night was already merging into the grey twilight of morning when I dismounted from my donkey at the Gur i Amir and bade the mulla good-bye. The town was beginning to wake up as I walked back into it on foot.

VII

Arrested!

As soon as I got back to the hotel I bade Khores get me some tea, and then lay down, hoping to sleep for hours. No such luck. Khores came to the door in great excitement to say that two militiamen were asking for me.

Flight would have been both senseless and dangerous. Only bluff could help in such a case, and bluff had proved on many previous occasions the goddess of my salvation.

I dressed and bade the gentlemen come in. Two Sart policemen entered and requested me to follow them to the Commission for Extraordinary Investigations, as Comrade Sorin wished to speak to me on pressing business. I was in the most unholy funk, but I tried to remain outwardly cool and unruffled, and said I should be delighted to come at once.

The offices of the G.P.U. were situated at the corner of the Katta Qurghan and Nikolayeffski Streets. The policemen led me into a room.

Comrade Sorin first asked me my name and the purpose of my visit to Samarqand. I gave him the desired information and in my turn requested to know the reason of my being summoned. He replied that every stranger who took quarters in an hotel was sent for as a matter of routine and invited to explain who he was and why he had come. I inwardly breathed a sigh of relief; then Sorin casually inquired whether I had ever been in Samarqand before. 'Yes, rather,' said I, 'why, I was a prisoner of war in the barracks of the Twelfth.' He then went on to ask whether I had worked in the Gorenberg Factory. To this, I said no; when the Communist

74

revolution came I had gone at once from the prison camp to join the Internationalists. Hereupon Sorin made a sign to one of the policemen and whispered something in his ear. The man went out and came back in a minute or two accompanied by Dosunyants. The commissar now turned to me.

'Do you know this comrade?'

'No!'

'Do you know an ex-prisoner of war named Krist?'

'No!'

'Comrade Dosunyants, do you know this foreign comrade?'

'Most emphatically yes! It is Comrade Krist, who was condemned in 1920 for counter-revolutionary activity.'

'Is that correct? Are you Krist?'

'I have already said that I am not. And I do not know this comrade here. This is the first time in my life that I have set eyes on him.'

'When were you demobilised from the Red Army?'

Now this was a tricky question, for I had never served in the Red Army at all. If I once gave the commissar a chance to cross-question me in detail, I was sunk. So I hastily answered:

'Immediately after the fighting round Qizil Arwat. I had been wounded, and as soon as I was let out of hospital I went to work in the railway workshops.'

'Where were you wounded, comrade?'

'In the thigh.' I pulled down my trouser and showed him the scar of the wound which I had got in 1914 on the San.

'And what are you now doing in Samarqand?'

'I have studied geology, and I want to prospect for minerals for Uzbegistan. If you care to make inquiries – you will find that I called on Comrade Babayeff yesterday to see about it, and that he has kindly promised to give me every assistance.'

'Have you any friends or acquaintances in the town?'

'Not a soul.'

'Inasmuch as Comrade Dosunyants believes that you are the ex-prisoner of war Krist, I must place you under arrest until the matter has been fully investigated. We shall treat you well. If it turns out, however, that you have been lying, and that you are here as a spy – then God have mercy on you.'

Sorin gave the policemen a written order and they led me away. I took pains not to betray how well I knew the town, but I was curious to see where they were going to take me to. We went up Katta Qurghan Street, then turned left down Gladbeshin Street, and halted a few minutes later in front of a small house where some Sart militia were on guard. My identification papers were taken from me in the office, and I was then led into the detention room, whose double benches were already well filled. I have never seen a more cosmopolitan crowd than was there assembled. There were Qirghiz, Sarts, Bukharan Jews, Turkomans, Armenians, Indians, Afghans, Gipsies, Persians, Tartars, with a few Chinese to complete the mixture. There must have been sixty of us in the tiny room, which was designed at most for twenty-five.

All too well acquainted as I was with the prisons of Turkistan, I knew the correct etiquette! I went to the end of one of the benches and shoved aside the Qirghiz who was lying on it, so that I got at least sitting room for myself. When they had searched me in the office they had confiscated nothing but my papers and my pistol, so that I had some money on me and could afford, if necessary, to buy myself food.

In the afternoon I was called into the office and two police again escorted me to the G.P.U. When I entered I saw Kerschbaum and three other old prisoner-of-war friends who had elected to stay on in Samarqand when the rest of us had made for home. They stared at me, but not by the twitch of an eyelid did any one of them betray that he had ever seen me before.

Sorin turned to the four friends: 'Comrades, Austrian ex-prisoners of war, do you know this man?'

'No!' they answered in chorus.

'Have you ever seen this comrade before?'

Again a simultaneous and quadruple 'No! My letter to Kersch-

76

baum had done its work well. All my friends had been warned in time.

Sorin now turned to me: 'Comrade Steinschneider, you are free and may return to your hotel. Comrade Dosunyants seems to have made a mistake when he thought he recognised you on the Abramoffsky Boulevard. I cordially beg your pardon, but you will admit that I took the trouble to clear the matter up as quickly as I could.'

I now begged the commissar to give me a statement of my release in writing, so that I could go and fetch my pistol. I also asked for a guide to take me to the guardhouse where I had been detained, as I was new to the town and might lose my way. The four Austrians gladly volunteered to show this kindness to a compatriot, and in this way we were able to go off together without attracting attention. I thanked my stars that the commissar was either too stupid or too lazy to make inquiries in Qizil Arwat. An answer from the Soviet authorities there that Steinschneider was in hospital might, in the circumstances, have cost me my life.

My friends and I went off together to a remote and modest little inn and talked for hours about old times and all we had been through together and everything that had happened in Samarqand since I had left. And my old comrades of the prison camp cross-questioned me in detail about home, which, as may be imagined, they all hungered after, despite their decision to remain in Tur-kistan.

Since it was the police themselves who had brought us together there was no further reason to avoid seeing each other. Kerschbaum invited me home to spend the evening with him. Then the others bade us good-bye, while Kerschbaum and I went off to the guard-house and recovered my pistol and *bumaga* without further formality.

That evening there was a great reunion in Kerschbaum's house. In addition to the four Austrians and their wives, we were joined by a Hungarian. I had to answer hundreds of questions about Austria and the post-war conditions there, and then hundreds

77

more. They all had entirely false ideas about conditions in Central Europe and in the victorious countries, for the Russian papers published the most confused and inaccurate news about Europe. Though it was now three years since I had left home myself, I was able to give a lot of information to my friends who had not been back since 1914, eleven years ago. When I said good-night to the dear fellows, time and we were alike far gone. The good Turkistan wine had produced a fine effect. One and all, however, were sober enough to give me the sound advice to make myself scarce at the first possible moment. Samarqand was distinctly unhealthy, but once I was out of sight of the authorities not a soul would bother his head about me. I thanked them warmly for all that they had done for me.

Safely back in my hotel I comforted the anxious Khores and lay down to sleep, for I had two lost nights to make up for.

Two days later I again called at the Soviet office, and to the honour of the god-almighty of Turkistan I must admit that everything was ready and waiting for me. Even a railway ticket had been supplied to carry me by Chernayevo and Khojand to Khoqand. A Government messenger was waiting in front of the railway station for me with the donkeys and the equipment I had indented for, while it had been arranged that the carriage and horse would be ready for me in Khoqand. I have seldom turned my back on any town so gladly as I did this time on Samarqand. The scare Dosunyants and the arrest had given me made me feel distinctly weak about the knees!

VIII

Across the Dengiz Bai

It was an unpleasant surprise to find on reaching Khoqand that the Soviet authorities had sent the cart, horse and supplies of fodder via Skobeleff to Sukhana on the Qizil Qaya railway, which branches off to the south about half-way between Khoqand and Andijan. I suggested that they might fetch the carriage back or else supply me with another, but they brusquely refused to do anything further in the matter. There was nothing to be done but to take the train to Gorchakovo, the junction for Sukhana. I had to wait three days till the train coughed its way slowly in. When at last we started I was so exhausted by the heat that I fell asleep in the carriage in spite of the racket made by my Sart fellow travellers. I woke up to my horror at Fechenko, having overshot my station. I didn't feel like waiting another three days for a return train to Gorchakovo, so I hired a carriage to do the twenty-five and a half miles back. When I got to Gorchakovo I found I was in luck for once, for a train was starting next day for Skobeleff and Qizil Qaya.

The small-gauge railway rattled through a barren valley southwards towards the Alai mountains. Ahead of us Mount Baba and the Zarafshan Glacier gleamed bright in the morning sun, and behind them rose the mighty summits of the Peter the Great range, some 23,000 feet high. After a run of about four hours our tiny train drew up in Sukhana. During the War some thousands of Austrians, Hungarians, and Germans had been sent to work in the Qizil Qaya coal-mines and hundreds of prisoners had died from hunger and sickness in the province of Farghana. The worst fate of all overtook the hundred and fifty Austrian prisoners of war who

took advantage of the native rising in Osh (in May 1919) to march
to Andijan in the hopes of getting on from there to Samarqand for
greater safety. A robber band of Sarts, under the leadership of Khoja
Khan, attacked the unarmed prisoners on the banks of the Sir Darya
and cut their throats, after subjecting them to the most gruesome
torture. They flung the bodies into the river and people living on
the bank told me that for days afterwards the river was carrying
down severed limbs of the hapless Austrians.

The cart was actually waiting for me in Sukhana. We loaded it
up with our supplies, a smart lad took on the job of driver, Khores
and I mounted our donkeys, and in the full midday heat our little
caravan set out for its unknown destination.

We intended to spend our first night in the village of Üch
Qurghan. The Alai range reared itself in front of us, almost
perpendicular cliffs rising straight out of the flat plain without a
break in their line to indicate a possible passage. The Izfairan shoots
into the plain through a dark and sinister ravine. Only a narrow
bridle track runs down alongside the torrent into the valley. High
in the mountain beside the Jatrabad rest hut a small deep-red
tributary flows into the Izfairan. It passes through a large deposit of
cinnabar on its way and takes the dye from it. On fine days its colour
is the brightest, most startling red, but the purity of the water seems
unaffected. After rain the colour changes to a dark red, and the
whole of the Izfairan looks like a river of blood.

It was dark before we reached Üch Qurghan, which lies in the
middle of a large fertile valley. We pitched our camp. The phrase
is too ambitious. We simply spread our blankets on the meadow
grass and camp was ready. Khores cooked a magnificent *pulau* and
we followed it by tea. The driver had tied the horse and the donkeys
to a tree and when our steed grew restless and tugged his rope, the
tree showered down juicy apricots on our heads, which we
devoured with much enjoyment.

Next morning we saw that we had lighted on a small, but
evidently prosperous Sart settlement. Rich corn-fields and orchards
surrounded our camp. There were even rice plantations, which

seemed in a thriving condition. Men and children soon gathered round us; we even saw an occasional veiled woman, but the new freedom seemed to have halted at the mountain frontier, and we saw no unveiled women such as we had met with in Samarqand and the other towns.

The *aqsaqal* of the village complained to me that herds of wild pig were laying waste his rice fields and begged me to shoot them. I gladly consented, and went with Khores to the rice fields, which were watered by irrigation channels from the Izfairan. As we reached the edge of the marsh we could already hear the grunting of the pigs and saw the damage they had caused amongst the rice, ripping it up with their snouts and trampling it down. Some Sart youths had come with us to act as beaters. They went round to the other side, behind the swine, and drove them towards us with loud cries. A few young pigs broke through first and we laid them low with well-aimed shots. Two large sows which came after their young met the same fate. Then with a great roar a large boar rushed out. I took aim and fired. I saw dust and dirt rise from the boar's hide as the shot hit him. He halted for a second and turned his head in my direction. I saw his treacherous eyes and his two mighty tusks. I tried to reload and repeat my shot but only an empty cartridge case spat out; the magazine was empty. The boar meanwhile had got on to firmer ground. He uttered a terrifying roar and charged at me. I leaped to one side hastily fitting a new magazine to my rifle. Before I could fire again he had stormed past and some one behind me uttered a cry. When I turned I saw Khores on the ground, and the boar tearing along twenty yards away. I raised my rifle and fired several shots after him. The brute crashed to the ground.

But Khores had received a ghastly wound. The charging boar had caught him with one of his tusks and ripped his leg open from knee to belly, exposing the bone. A great stream of blood was pouring from the wound. I cut off his trouser and tore it into strips, with which I bandaged the injured leg. With the help of the Sarts I carried the half-conscious man back to camp. I tore up all my

81

spare linen for bandages, which I bound tightly round the leg. We spread all the blankets on the carriage and a sad little procession retraced its steps to Qizil Qaya.

The Russian mining doctor at once took Khores under his care and praised my prompt efforts at first aid. We got the wounded man into the shelter of a hut. But two days afterwards my friend was dead.

After this tragic accident I seriously wondered whether it would not be better to give up the whole adventure and return to Persia. But on reflection I could see no advantage in that to any one. Nothing I did or left undone could bring poor Khores back to life, and the greater part of my plan would remain unfulfilled. I sent back the driver and the cart and decided to go on alone. I packed my kit on the one donkey and kept the other as a mount for myself. Once again my two asses and I trotted off, out of Qizil Qaya and towards the mountains. I was now quite alone. I begged the Russian doctor to send Khores' possessions to Alim Qul, who, in his *aul* over a thousand miles away, must have received the news of his son's death with grief and sorrow.

Just as night was falling I rode again into Üch Qurghan and spent the night in the *chai-khana*.

Forbidding and inhospitable as the Izfairan looks where it issues from its gorge into the plain, it proves rich and fertile in its upper reaches. The ravine opens out into a valley; richly cultivated fields and fruit gardens alternate with luscious meadows on which camels, donkeys, horses, sheep, and cows graze. The path repeatedly crosses the river on the most primitive type of bridge, consisting simply of logs loosely thrown across. I was often obliged to tie the donkeys on a rope, cross the tottering bridge myself on foot and then drag the unwilling beasts across with all my might, while the Izfairan roared below us at incredible speed.

On the second day I reached the village of Qara'ul, round which there had been very heavy fighting when the Russians first attempted to march into the province of Bukhara. Just before the *qishlaq* we came to a more than usually sketchy bridge which the donkeys absolutely refused to face. Nothing would induce them to trust themselves to the spindly branches. Following my established procedure I tied them to a rope, went over myself, threw a rope around a juniper, and tugged with all my might. I succeeded in getting the pig-headed brutes on the bridge all right, but they stuck out their legs stiffly and resisted with all their strength. I untied one and led him back to the original bank, hoping to be able to manipulate them one at a time. The single donkey could not hold out against me and I dragged him to about the middle of the bridge, where he succeeded in digging himself in again. An extra strong tug on my part and the rotten wood gave way. The donkey fell through and dangled between bridge and water. Try as I might I could not haul the poor beast up again. To go on half an hour's march to the village for help would have been no use, for the odds were a thousand to one that the donkey would meantime have strangled himself on the rope. I tore a log out of the bridge, placed it at right angles across the breach, and fastened one end of the rope to it. Then, using a technique which I had often practised in the Austrian Alps, I climbed down the rope to the luckless donkey. With the greatest difficulty I got the loading saddle off him and brought it to safety. Then I drew my knife and cut the rope on which he was suspended. I felt sad to see my four-footed comrade disappear in the Izfairan torrent, which speedily swirled the struggling grey body out of sight. The next business was to repair the bridge as best I might, and lead the remaining animal across, which I succeeded in doing after many hours of hard work.

Cheerful new mud houses had replaced the ruined huts of Qara'ul which had been shattered in the bombardment. These new buildings had, it is true, no windows, only simple holes in the wall that could be closed with wooden shutters, but the rooms were whitewashed inside and kept clean.

Central Asian architecture, especially in Turkistan and Bukhara, is as old as the hills and simplicity itself. There are no foundations in our sense of the term. In front of the site on which the proposed house is to be built they dig a trench, into which water is allowed

83

to pour constantly. A wooden mould is used to shape the wet mud into bricks, which are dried in the sun, while more mud serves in a second capacity as mortar. When the walls are about nine and a half feet high, thin, untrimmed poles of silver poplar are laid across them. Mats of reeds or straw are now placed over these slightly sloping rafters and the roof is completed by a layer of mud over a foot thick. This mud is mixed with finely chopped straw to give it a firmer consistency.

The soil in these regions is mainly loess and it becomes so hard in the heat of the sun that within a few months it is better able to resist wind and weather than stone or burnt brick. Such houses are often several centuries old. The original trench which furnished the building material is by no means wasted. Filled with water it provides the indispensable tank or pond for the future house and garden. This *hauz* supplies water for washing and cooking as well as for watering flowers and trees. All through the summer the natives spend their nights and their daytime leisure on the brink of the *hauz*. Here they sleep, drink their tea, and eat their meals. They often build a light balcony with thin poles on the flat roof and cover it with reed mats. This *bala-khana* is reached by a primitive ladder and serves as a guest-room for visitors who come to stay for any length of time.

Several channels are led off from the *hauz*, which serve for irrigation. The material dug out when constructing these serves to build the walls which surround every Sart house. They may be as high as fifteen or sixteen feet, and prevent passers-by from prying into the private life of the family. Door and window-frames are unknown – the hinges for the wooden shutters are built straight into the wall. A room has usually only one opening, which serves both as door and window. In winter and during the rains, when the shutters are necessarily closed, the room is completely dark. Artificial lighting is provided by candles, and in more sophisticated places by oil-lamps, but often by home-made oil-cruses such as were used in ancient Greece and Rome. A simple earthen dish is filled with cotton oil and a twist of cotton supplies the floating wick.

Diagram of a Turkistan House

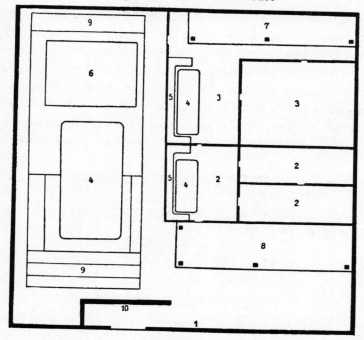

PLAN

1. Surrounding wall, thirteen to sixteen feet high.
2. Harem, or women's quarters.
3. Men's quarters.
4. Tanks (*Hauz*).
5. Raised benches of mud.
6. Raised terrace of mud.
7. Stables.
8. Covered terrace for women.
9. Trenches for water.
10. Inner curtain wall screening entrance to enclosure.

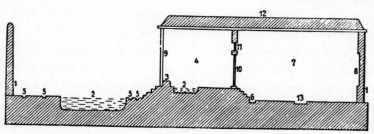

SECTION

1. Surrounding wall.
2. Tanks.
3. Raised benches.
4. Covered terrace.
5. Trenches for water.
6. Sunk trough for outdoor shoes.
7. Living-room.
8. Niche for clothing.
9. Wooden pillars supporting roof of terrace.
10. Doors.
11. Wooden shutters (windows)
12. Mud roof.
13. Sunk fireplace for charcoal stove (*manqal*).

85

The cold weather lasts on an average three months. Stoves are unknown. As a protection against the cold, men and women put on padded cloaks over their usual summer clothes. Those who are better off wrap themselves in fur cloaks, but these are costly luxuries. When the family is indoors the *manqal*, or basin of charcoal, is placed in the centre of the room. Over it a table-like iron framework is placed, from which padded quilts hang down to the ground. The members of the family crouch round the *manqal*

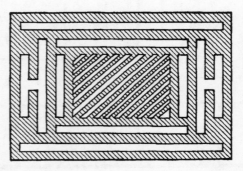

Window of wooden lattice work, such as is usual in Bukhara

on several thicknesses of felt carpet placed on the earthen floor – wooden floors are quite unknown – and draw the padded quilts over them. The cave-like retreat thus formed in the centre is pleasantly warmed by the burning charcoal, and the poisonous fumes are carried off by a central opening in the roof. Within easy reach stands the ever-boiling samovar, whose tea supplies the body with central heat. In this way Sarts, Bukharans, Qirghiz, and Turkomans defend themselves as best they may against the rigours of winter.

Where the gate breaks the line of the court wall an inner curtain-wall several yards wide is built, so that even when the gate has to be opened to a stranger he will get no peep into the privacy of the interior.

Even the poorest house is divided into two. The smaller side is usually allotted to the women for their harem and cannot be entered from the rest of the house. The harem possesses an entirely closed-in court and garden of its own, and communicates by one door with the terrace belonging to the master of the house. If a visitor comes and wife or daughter happens to be in the men's part of the house, the caller is simply kept waiting at the door until the coast is clear.

In the towns and the larger oases of Turkistan Communist and anti-god propaganda have possibly modified the people's customs

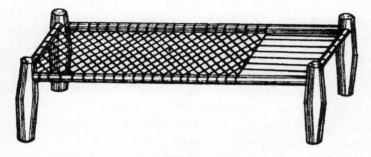

Turkistan bedstead. The wooden frame is lashed from side to side and from end to end with ropes of camel- and horse-hair. The use of bedsteads is confined to the wealthy

a little, but the new doctrines have as yet had little or no effect in the villages and towns of eastern Bukhara. Not in vain has the province of Bukhara been for centuries the fortress of Islam. Outside the big towns, and more especially among the nomads, habits and customs have remained unchanged for centuries.

In southern Bukhara the methods of building are still simpler than those I have described. There they make great balls of mud, pile them up, and stamp them down with their feet. When one layer has dried out the next is placed on top. The Bukharans claim that none of the frequent earthquakes that occur in these regions has ever been known to knock down a house built of mud, while more ambitious buildings crumble like a house of cards at the first tremor.

This type of architecture has become customary throughout Turkistan primarily because the lack of fuel makes it impossible to fire brick, and the lack of timber makes taller houses impracticable. Probably a contributory reason is that the inhabitants frequently change their dwelling place, and must be in a position to build new houses in a short time in their new settlement. Quintus Curtius records that Alexander the Great built 27,000 houses and the city wall of Alexandria on the Tanaïs (the Khojand of to-day) in seventeen days. It is a remarkable fact that the mosques, madrasahs, and many of the public baths dating from Timur's time were carried out in thin burnt brick. Stone buildings are found only in the mountains of eastern Bukhara and in Farghana, in Darwaz, Badakhshan, and a few other places. In ancient times the inhabitants of Turkistan must have been largely cave-dwellers, as is proved by the gigantic caves that have been found near Samarqand, Qarshi, Kerki, and Merv; entire subterranean towns of considerable extent have been excavated from the loess soil. Of course it is possible that these were places in which the people took refuge only when powerful enemies threatened the town.

It is obvious that under the primitive conditions I have described winter takes a heavy toll of life in Turkistan. Thermometers are of course unknown, and the natives reckon the varying degree of cold by the numbers of luckless folk frozen inside the house during a given winter. The Sarts still talk with horror of the winter of 1912, in which some 3,000 people were frozen to death in their own homes in Bukhara alone.

All that I have said above applies also to the dwellings of the well to do, except in so far as they live in the larger oases which have borrowed some features of Russian civilisation. I once stayed a night in the house of the ex-Beg of Faizabad. It was a one-story building with fully sixteen rooms, but not one of these boasted either a window or a stove. The only sign of luxury I saw was a large hall whose roof was supported on a number of beautifully carved and painted pillars, while the floor was fairly smothered under a mass of costly silk carpets. The Beg's greatest pride was a lantern made of common tin, like the old-fashioned gas lanterns we used to have for lighting the streets. This contained an oil-lamp. Yet my host was considered one of the richest men in eastern Bukhara, and that means something, for the numerous nobles used to possess very considerable wealth.

In Qara'ul I was able to buy cheap, a successor to my drowned donkey and I again took the road, which now climbed steeply up in a series of zigzags. As far as Qara'ul the road had been kept in some sort of half-repair; it now became narrower and vastly worse. As night began to draw on I came to a newly built house which gave an impression of great cleanliness. It was surrounded by a high wall. The road wound on above it in such a way that I was able to look down and see in; there seemed to be no one inside. Perhaps I could spend the night there. I tethered my donkeys to a rock and went back to the entrance. After much energetic knocking on my part, a small peephole in the door was cautiously opened from inside and the barrel of a rifle shot out while a voice commanded the stranger to be gone at once or the owner would shoot. I immediately sprang close in under the door so as not to offer a target, and from this vantage point I started negotiations with my invisible host. I told him I was a Government geologist, sorely in need of a rest, for which reason I should be grateful for a night's shelter. Naturally I was prepared to pay for everything. With some ungracious grunting the door was opened. I fetched my donkeys along and showed the Tajik my papers, which he examined with the utmost care. He was obviously reassured, for he led my beasts at once to the stable and threw down some straw for them to eat. Not till this was done did he invite me to follow him into the house.

My host proved to be an *archa-chik*, namely a guardian of the juniper, who had been posted here to try to save the scanty timber from being completely destroyed. Two years ago the Soviet of Uzbegistan had sent twenty-one such forest officers into this part of the Alai mountains and had built them houses in various places at State expense. The juniper is the only tree which flourishes in the mountains of Bukhara. In the Alai and in the Hisar ranges the juniper thrives up to a height of 13,000 feet, where it even forms whole forests. The once ample supply of timber on the northern slopes of the Alai had been sorely thinned out during the Great War and later during the Civil War, for this hard and gnarled wood yields the very best charcoal. On the southern face of the Alai there are forests of walnut whose greatest value is their disease. A morbid excrescence on the tree provides a valuable wood for carving. It is exported to America, and according to local report one tree may fetch as much as 10,000 gold roubles – a statement I accept with due reservation. The *archa* looks not unlike our fir and reaches a maximum height of about sixty feet and a diameter of over a yard at the base. In the Pamirs at over 13,000 feet I saw surviving only low, tormented specimens scarcely over three feet high.

The forest officers had been appointed to protect this valuable stock of timber – for the juniper takes eighty years to reach its full development. As there are no other trees on the northern side of the mountains, and as furthermore charcoal is absolutely necessary to life, groups of ten or fifteen woodmen each were formed to search the mountains and collect any trees which had been uprooted by avalanches of stones or snow, or which had been blown over by storms. With endless toil they dragged these casualties down to the valley, where they set up their charcoal kilns.

The forest officers have the right to shoot at sight any one whom they catch in the act of felling a living tree. These worthy men are naturally in bad odour with the inhabitants of the high *qishlaqs* and with the nomads crossing the mountains, since they prevent their getting free supplies of charcoal, to which they have considered themselves entitled from time immemorial. The forest officers have to be constantly on their guard against attack, hence the ready rifle with which my host had greeted my arrival.

Long after we were comfortably stretched out on our felt bedding and the primitive oil-lamp was out, the guardian of junipers went on spinning me yarns about the dangers, hardships, and adventures of his life, well content for once to have a sympathetic listener.

Once upon a time, on the very site where the forester's house now stands, there had been a *rabat*, or rest-house, which the Khan of Khoqand had built as a protection for the caravans which every year crossed the Dengiz Bai from Bukhara into Farghana or vice versa. Their camels carried valuable loads of gold, turquoise, carpets, silk, tobacco, wool, corn, and weapons. Many of these caravans were seen in Qara'ul or in Daraut Qurghan respectively, but failed to arrive at their destination. They simply evaporated. The Russian governor in Tashkent, or the Bukharan Diwan Begi, whichever it might be, made inquiries into the mysterious disappearance of the caravans and their treasure, but all were fruitless.

Not until the Russians conquered Bukhara in 1920 was the riddle solved. One of the places which offered the sturdiest resistance to the Russian advance was this *rabat* on whose floor we were now lying. It was the scene of long and bitter fighting, and it was only taken after much bloodshed on both sides. The *rabat-bashi* and his surviving servants were carried off to Skobeleff and brought before the Revolutionary Tribunal. During his trial the *bashi*, who knew that in any case his life was forfeit, proudly boasted that he had murdered at least four hundred and eleven men in his caravanserai. His uncle, the bandit-chief Khoja Khan, would send his retainers by secret tracks through ravines of the Turkistan mountains which were known to no one but themselves, to drive off the camels with their costly loads, while he himself disposed of the people in charge. His procedure was ingenious. He entertained the newly arrived guests with drink, including always tarantula schnapps. When they were thoroughly drunk on this poisoned liquor he threw them into the cellar to feed his bear. He used to keep the bear for weeks without other food till it was reconciled to human flesh.

After this gruesome confession, a detachment of the Red Army was sent back into the mountains and – sure enough – under the ruins of the bombarded caravanserai they found the cellar with a great savage bear and the bones of hundreds of its victims covering the floor in thick layers. The lost valuables were never recovered. The old man told me that every day he searched about in the neighbourhood hoping to find that some of the gold or jewels had been buried.

I asked particulars about the tarantula schnapps. He told me that this drink had been known and used in Turkistan from time immemorial. If you want to brew it you catch a number of the poisonous spiders, put them in a glass, and throw in some scraps of dried apples or apricots. The furious brutes fling themselves on the food and bite into it. They thus inject their poison into the dry fruit, which you then mix with fermented grapes. Thirty or forty tarantulas make about a quart of the deadly brew. A tiny glass of this liqueur is enough to drive a man insane. Half an hour after he has drunk it the victim is so paralysed that he cannot move; an hour later he is raving mad.

The caretaker of the caravanserai used to dope his guests with this tarantula schnapps, and as soon as paralysis set in he threw them to the bear, who did the rest. The Russians condemned the man to death, but in the night the Sarts broke into the prison and fetched him out into the desert. They tied him with ropes to the saddles of two swift camels, stuffed pepper in their behinds so that the infuriated animals dashed out into the desert dragging the body of the hundredfold murderer after them. A few days later his skeleton was found, picked clean by the vultures.

I listened with great interest to the old man's tales. He had been born in the mountains and reared amongst robbers. He frankly admitted that he had formerly belonged to Madamin Beg's bandit gang and had later fought with Enver against the Reds. I listened eagerly, thinking I might at last get the final truth about Enver Pasha's death. My host was dropping off to sleep by now and in answer to my questions murmured: 'Next time you get to Deh i Nau, ask Agabekoff. He knows better than any one.'

Next morning I set out uphill once more along the banks of the Izfairan. Singing birds of every sort were twittering in the branches of the junipers. The rain had apparently wakened them to new life, for there had been none to be heard before. I had met neither nomads nor goods caravans since I had left Qizil Qaya. The mountain plateau was silent and deserted. The loess had now given place to pure rock. Every now and then I heard the thunder-like

The population of Chikoi is one of the most mixed in Asia. I asked one man to raise his hand that I might focus my camera. They all responded to my request

roar of a stone-avalanche in the distance. As the sun mounted, its burning rays poured vertically down into my narrow gorge, and in a twinkling dew and rain dried up. At noon I halted for a rest, cooked a little rice in mutton fat, and took a dip in the ice-cold water of the torrent. I had taken off my clothes and shoes and resumed my pilgrimage as naked as Father Adam. I wanted to continue the march until I had found a suitable camping-place.

Night had fallen. My two donkeys stopped at intervals, as if to remind me that it was high time for bed. Soon the moon rose and the high-lying glaciers gleamed with milk-white magic light. The gorge opened out a little, stones and boulders merged into grass, and presently I saw lights ahead. I slipped on my cloak and went up to the first house. The owner led me along to the *chai-khana* and on inquiry I learned that I had reached the little *qishlaq* of Chikoi.

The next day was bitter. Yesterday I had been marching naked even after sundown. Today I put on my two padded cloaks one on top of the other and still was nearly frozen. Not till midday when the road, which had climbed steadily up, was some 750 feet above the river, and the sun shone straight down into the narrow crack of my ravine, was it warm enough for me to take the cloaks off and throw them on the donkey's back again. High above me there was a more than life-size human figure in ancient-looking dress, carved in the rock. I tethered the donkeys and climbed up to examine the giant relief. I knocked off a few specimens of the adjacent rock and found it was of an extra hard type of stone, yet the figure had suffered seriously from weathering. All sharp edges had been rounded off and parts of it had cracked. In places where it was sheltered from the wind, the original form had been preserved uninjured. It must have been hundreds of years since some Mongol or Uzbeg artist had here exercised his skill. What strange impulse had prompted him to choose this remote and lonely mountain track?

As evening drew on, I heard the notes of a horn and I soon found myself standing in front of an almost wholly ruined mill. The miller's living-room was in a cave below the water-wheel and he was glad enough to share it with me. He complained that for the last few years custom had been very slack. In olden days dozens of caravans crossed the Dengiz Bai every day in summer, but since Soviet rule had come the route was being less and less used, and the nomads had betaken themselves into Chinese Turkistan, where they enjoyed more freedom. The caravans always used to carry grain and rice for the journey and none of them would pass without getting some flour ground for themselves in his mill.

The miller warned me that about an hour's march farther on the Izfairan had carried away the bridge, and that I should have some trouble in getting myself and my animals across the river. At my request he came with me to the place, and plunging breast high into the raging water he carried my donkeys across one by one on his shoulders! I offered him five roubles for his trouble, but he refused them with a laugh, saying that Allah would one day reward him, for the Quran enjoined on every man to offer help to travellers. I had difficulty in persuading him to accept even a handful of Farghana tobacco, though this must have been a welcome and costly rarity to him.

After the non-existent bridge the road widened and developed into a regular highway. I heard later in Jidinji that this part of the road had been built in 1916 and 1917 by Austrian and Hungarian prisoners of war from Skobeleff. It was designed to follow the Izfairan all the way to Qizil Qaya, but it was never finished. The Communist Revolution came and war broke out between the bands of Sarts and Tajiks. Not far from Surmach a Qirghiz showed me a small graveyard in which thirty-seven Austrians and Hungarians are buried; they had been killed by accidents or died of sickness when working on the road. So even here, at a height of close on 10,000 feet, in this most remote corner of the Russian Empire, and close to the Chinese frontier, victims of the World War are sleeping their last sleep. A few simple wooden crosses bore illegible inscriptions; I was not able to decipher even the names of the dead. I stood for a long time in front of the tumbled-in graves of my fellow countrymen who had been fated to die nearly 4,000 miles from home.

Before long I struck the first advance posts of the Qara Qirghiz and my further wanderings led me through their grazing territories. Donkeys, horses, and camels supply their only means of subsistence. The mares' milk yields their beloved *qumiz*, one of the mainstays of life both to nomads and mountain-dwellers.

95

The milk is filled into sheepskins and rocked about until it ferments and becomes thick and buttery. Camels' and sheep's milk provide the scarcely less beloved *airan*, which, in the mountains, is eaten mixed with snow or ice. The Qara Qirghiz know nothing of butter-making, which is practised only in the oases and the lower valleys.

I put in two days' rest here to refresh myself and my asses. I should have been only too glad to linger longer in so idyllic a spot. As soon as the Qirghiz were convinced that I was no Bolshevist they showed me the greatest confidence and hospitality, and a sheep was slaughtered and roasted in my honour. I watched the preparations for a festive feed with acute interest. A deep trench was dug and almost completely filled with juniper wood, which was then set on fire. When nothing but glowing coals remained, a log was laid across, to the under side of which the cleaned carcass of the sheep was slung. The trench was then completely covered in with earth and branches. About two hours later the perfectly roasted sheep was taken out and divided. The *aqsaqal* and I, as the guests of honour, were each allotted a hind leg, while the balance of the meat was shared between the remaining nine. In less time than it takes to tell, the eleven of us – including some children – had polished off the whole of a fairly large sheep. Enormous earthen jars of *qumiz* and *airan* were dragged to the fore and disposed of almost as quickly.

For the last twenty years the Qirghiz of the steppes had been more or less under the domination of the Russians; not so the Qirghiz of the mountains. On the northern slopes of the Greater and Lesser Alai, in the Great Alai Valley, and on the Pamirs the Qara Qirghiz have continued to live the same independent existence as their forebears in the days of the Golden Horde. Subject to no man, free of all taxes and all restrictions, they trek through the country with their flocks at their own sweet will. If I was to get to know the genuine Qirghiz life I must push on into the valley of the Alai. Who knows, thought I, how long their freedom there will last? Perhaps in ten, perhaps in twenty years, the victorious march of western civilisation will have destroyed the last traces of their natural nomad life.

The Qirghiz are divided into two: the Qirghiz Qazaq and the Qara (Black) Qirghiz. The Qazaq – who have of course no connection whatever with 'Cossacks' – range from the Volga to the Ebi Nor in Dzungaria and from Afghanistan to Siberia, while the Qara Qirghiz consider the mountains of Turkistan and western China as their hereditary grazing grounds. The greater bulk of the Black Qirghiz, numbering perhaps 300,000 souls, live in the Alai, the Farghana mountains, and the Pamirs. They profess themselves Sunni Muhammadans, but are not unduly afflicted with religion. Ceremonial ablutions, prayers, and Quranic observances are as good as unknown amongst them. What they associate with Muhammad's teaching is the ceremony of circumcision, the shaving of the men's heads, and a passion for religious legends and fairy stories, to which they listen with delight. For the rest, they are superstitious in a very high degree. Their *baqsis* (medicine men or magician-priests) exercise a great deal more influence on their everyday life than even the most respected mullas. Contrary to Quranic injunction, their women go about unveiled. The reason of this may be that their wandering life permits them no mosques or madrasahs where they could hear the Quran expounded or be exhorted to follow its teachings.

The magician-priests are their doctors, and are supposed to banish ill luck, conjure good fortune, and control the weather. To keep up their prestige they walk on glowing iron, eat burning charcoal, and swallow nails, whips, and broken glass. From ashes and bones they foretell the future, and they brew magic draughts for the miscellaneous contingencies of human life.

Despite the sketchiness of their religion, the morals of the Qirghiz are very high. They are honourable and faithful. Their hospitality is exceeded only by that of the Yomut Turkomans. They have no shadow of piety towards the dead. Now and then you come across the mound of a Qirghiz saint, decorated with horse-tails; you can then be very sure that it marks the grave of a powerful magician or a famous *batir*. A *batir* is a cattle-thief who has accumulated riches by his skill in stealing horses. His grateful heirs then erect a grave mound, or even a mud mausoleum, to his honoured memory. Robbery and horse-stealing, when committed against another tribe, are considered a virtue rather than a crime, a fact perfectly consistent with the lofty code of honour above mentioned. Except where they come in contact with the law as administered by State judges in civilised centres their legal code is well adapted to their philosophy of life. They never willingly seek redress in ordinary law courts, but prefer the judgement of their own tribal assemblies. The highest penalty that can be imposed is a *qun*, namely a fine of five hundred sheep, fifty horses, and twenty-five camels; this serves also as the unit of punishment. According to the gravity of the offence, a whole, half, or quarter *qun* is imposed. The whole family of the offender, the whole *aul*, even the whole tribe, is responsible for paying up the fine. If a man is condemned because of a theft he must not only restore the stolen property and pay the fine, but forfeit his own weapons and clothes to the family of his victim.

The whole wealth of the Qirghiz lies in their flocks and herds, to which they owe everything they possess. They weave clothes and carpets from the hair of their camels, and they also trample it out to make their felt rugs, which they need to hang round the walls of their yurts and to spread over the floor. In districts where timber is scarce they dry camel and ass dung to make the fuel with which their yurts are heated through the winter. Carts are un-known, and all their goods are carried about on camels, which are much stronger than the African or Persian camel. A load of four to five hundredweight is the average, and with this a Qirghiz camel will cheerfully march thirty to forty miles a day. Though they keep large numbers of horses they use them only for hunting or playing games on horseback. When they are on the move the herds of horses follow the march unladen.

They have immense numbers of sheep of the fat-tailed kind, the tails of which yield on an average 30 or 40 lbs. of fat each. There are families who possess 20,000 head of sheep and more, while their stock of cows is very small. Where the height of the grazing and camping grounds runs to over 6,000 feet, yaks are the usual beasts of burden. These yaks are of Tibetan breed; they are coal black and look most sinister and terrifying. Their looks belie them, however, for they are in fact quite harmless and extraordinarily good tempered. No other mammal gives milk so good or with so high a fat-content, but they can only be kept at, or above, a height of 6,000 feet. At lower altitudes they perish.

After my two days' rest I quitted Langar, 6,600 feet above sea-level. Light snow had fallen during the night but the Turkistan sun had melted it again before midday. The road now mounted between dark rock walls and lofty juniper woods alongside the roaring Izfairan. The uncanny red rock cliffs are so steep and high that it is only when the sun reaches its zenith that any sunlight penetrates these deep gorges.

The side valleys of the Alai now become larger and more frequent. At the little hamlet of Jatrabad the red river I mentioned above flows in from one of the side valleys and dyes the Izfairan for the whole of its course to the valley far below. I left my baggage and my two donkeys in the *chai-khana* at Jatrabad, to go and explore the valley of the red river. After about an hour's march it widened out into a rich and well-watered meadow where a large nomad family of a hundred yurts or so had pitched their camp. A three hours' march brought me to the place where the unnamed stream acquired its colour. Above this spot a bright, clear spring gives birth to a pure crystal waterfall, which tumbles into the valley to flow through a stretch of brilliantly red earth over three hundred yards wide. The water must absorb enormous quantities of this red soil, but without appearing to diminish its mass. In order to be able to justify my existence as a State geologist – in case the authorities should later make any inquiry into my pursuits – I took some samples of the red earth with me. It is amazing with what riches Mother Nature has endowed the mountain world of Turkistan. This one tiny valley contains millions and millions of pounds of the purest natural mineral dye, absolutely ready for use! There must also be quantities of mercury in the immediate neighbourhood, for this is always found in close conjunction with cinnabar. On the way back to Jatrabad four great eagles rose so close in front of me that the wind from their wings swept across my face. They had their eyrie on a jutting cliff many hundred feet above. They flew up and alighted on it, gazing down with astonishment on the human intruder who had disturbed their peace.

Next morning I resumed my climb towards the *chai-khana* of Jidinji, the last rest-house of any kind before the actual pass itself. The wails of rock tower up a full 3,000 feet and the narrow precarious track winds up their face in countless zigzags. I reached the snow line just before Jidinji and when I got to the *chai-khana* I found it deep in snow. It was crowded with people, for a large Qirghiz caravan coming up from the Alai valley was halting here to rest before engaging on the downward march into Farghana. A few groups of Tajiks from the Qara Tegin region were also in possession. They had come on foot from Khoqand and were returning to their own mountains. Next morning I rose bright and early for my final assault on the pass. Late the night before yet another caravan, laden with rice and cotton, had arrived; it was also bound for the Dengiz Bai, en route for Daraut Qurghan. I attached myself to it and we started off together.

After an hour's going the valley widened greatly into a high plateau. We were soon in the middle of a strange snow-landscape unaccountably decorated with long icicles. When the sun topped Mount Kauffmann (today known as Mount Lenin) and flooded its snowfields and glaciers with rosy light, I recognised that these bunches of icicles concealed bushes of dwarf juniper – a very forest of them, of considerable extent. After leaving the juniper woods behind us, the Qirghiz turned off into a side valley and halted on the bank of the Iskandar Kul – the Lake of Alexander. Oddly enough, there are no less than five Lakes of Alexander in Turkistan, and each of them claims to have seen Alexander the Great camping beside its waters. Our lake was stiff with fish; it almost looked as if it were used as an artificial hatchery. I marvelled at this, and the Qirghiz explained that it was a holy lake. Any impious person who ventured to eat one of the sacred fish would inevitably die.

When the Qirghiz marched off again I purposely remained behind, not to hurt their susceptibilities by letting them see me catch one of the fishes of the holy lake. I made a fishing net out of a handkerchief and soon had a small fish, seven or eight inches long, flapping about in it. I killed it, wrapped it in snow, and folded it in a cloth. Later I dried it in the sun without gutting it and months afterwards I gave it to a Balti doctor in Charjui. I told him my story of the holy lake and he set about to analyse my catch. While doing so he thoughtlessly threw the dried innards out of the window into the courtyard, where his watchdog greedily devoured them. Half an hour later the unfortunate animal died after the most dreadful howling. The doctor honoured him with a post mortem and diagnosed heart-failure due to some unknown poison which had also caused decomposition of the blood. This revealed the secret of the holy lake and its sacred fish. Granted the deep-rooted superstitions of the Turkistan natives, it is not to be wondered at that after a few people had died as a consequence of eating these poisonous fish, they should have dubbed the lake 'holy'.

The road on was one of toil and strain, for my feet sank in at almost every step. At last, about four in the afternoon, we reached the pass at a height of some 12,500 feet. The last 600 or 700 feet of climbing over an immense moraine was a severe tax on the lungs. Giddiness and headache accompanied the mountain sickness. The pass itself is a cleft between steep rock walls which cut off any immediate view. When I struck along the track to the right, after getting free of the rock wall, the sight that met my eyes was all the more overwhelming. There was a clear and distant view away to south and east and west. In the south-east towered the mighty peaks of the lofty Pamir plateau, the so-called Roof of the World. Lifting its glaciers and its fields of ice like gigantic magic fortresses to heaven. In the east the summit of Mount Kauffmann, 23,386 feet high, glimmered a blueish white, with Qizil Aghin alongside it on the left; from west to east ran the great chain of the Trans-Alai. In the north-east rose Mount Baba, 19,500 feet, the highest point of the Alai. In the west, like a blue-green ribbon the great ice-field of the Zarafshan glacier wound its way downwards to the valley below.

Late that night I reached the small, half-ruined mud village of Artaq, which is already across the border in the province of Qara Tegin. I had some difficulty in finding shelter in the *chai-khana*. Every self-respecting bandit would protest if I damned the rest-house of Artaq as a den of robbers. I have spent the night in many filthy and questionable holes in the course of my wanderings, but the *chai-khana* of Artaq easily heads the list. The *chai-khana-chik* shared his only room with his donkeys, sheep, and hens. To mitigate the savage cold to some extent a great fire of juniper was blazing in the centre of the room, and despite the many gaps in roof and walls its biting smoke could only very partially escape, and my eyes watered continually. I should have preferred to pitch camp in the open but the cold was too severe. With my contribution of two donkeys we had altogether four donkeys, three sheep and a dozen hens in the wretched hole of eight or nine square yards. To spread out my bedding I had to sweep aside the animals' dung. This greatly surprised my Qirghiz host, who assured me that donkey dung was far the best preventive of lice and bugs.

A caravan road runs north-east from Daraut Qurghan through the valley of the Qizil Su, which is twelve or thirteen miles wide. At the height of about 9,000 feet the road divides. One branch leads via Gulcha to Andijan, the other via Irkishtam to Kashgar in Chinese Turkistan, crossing in its path the Tüyä Murun Pass at over 11,000 feet. It is interesting to note that the Qizil Su changes its name when it leaves Turki-speaking territory; in Bukharan territory, after being joined by the Muk Su, it adopts the Persian name of Surkh Ab, both names in their respective languages describing it as Crimson Water. As the Surkh Ab it ultimately flows into the Amu Darya, Mother of Rivers.

I was now free to choose. I could either take the road towards the north-east, through the Alai valley by Sari Tash and the Qizil Art Pass up on to the Pamir plateau and thence reach the province of Bukhara again passing the Qara Kul, or on the other hand I could follow the Qizil Su downstream and get to Bukhara via Qurghan Tübe. In spite of the lateness of the season, I chose the first and longer route, up the Qizil Su, because it was unknown to me.

I again allowed myself a two-day halt in Daraut Qurghan both to get my pretty tattered wardrobe put into some sort of order and to take some sorely needed rest.

IX

Through the Alai Valley on to the Pamirs

A fairly good caravan road leads upstream along the Qizil Su, between the Alai and the Trans-Alai ranges. It mounts pretty steadily through the loveliest valley in Asia. On the left the high rock cliffs of the Alai plunge steeply down into the valley, while on the opposite side, the right, rise the wooded mountain sides, to change presently into the precipices and ice-fields of the Trans-Alai.

The valley itself is a stretch of flowery alpine meadow of inconceivable beauty. Though the steep rock faces on the left were covered deep in snow, rare flowers of every brilliant colour bloomed in profusion amidst the grass at their base. Hundreds and hundreds of black Qirghiz yurts dotted the pastures, camels and yaks grazed peacefully side by side, flocks of innumerable sheep scrambled like chamois amongst the cliffs and rocks, while troops of tiny horse-herds drove their charges to the river to water them.

Here is the last stronghold of Qirghiz freedom. The Qara Qirghiz have most unjustly won a place in literature as wild and savage nomads. They are not unlike their own yaks, sinister and terrifying enough to look at, but just as good natured and harmless on a nearer acquaintance. They take the wandering stranger into their tents with eager hospitality, so long as he respects their habits and obeys their laws. The remoteness and inaccessibility of their country has so far protected them from being conquered either by Bukharans or by Russians, and has shielded them from contact with the latter's civilisation – much to the advantage of the Qara Qirghiz!

Years before, in 1919 to be exact, some Austrians had found

their way over the Dengiz Bai into the Alai valley. They had escaped from prison camps in Farghana and were hoping to make their way through the province of Bukhara into Afghanistan and thence home. Amongst them was a German, Schaufuss, from the Sudeten mountain country. Some thirty of them started out on the perilous journey; only four ever reached their goal. The others either succumbed to hardship and exertion or were attacked, robbed, and murdered. The feats of heroism these prisoners of war accomplished border on the miraculous, but no chronicler has told their tale. With a few handfuls of rice and dried apricots, without map or compass, insufficiently clad and shod, penniless except for a few Romanoff roubles in their pockets, and ignorant of the local languages, they challenged the Alai.

What a contrast between their grim adventure and the grandiose expedition undertaken by the Germans under Rickmers, who traversed the Alai and the Pamirs a few years after me! It consisted of twenty-five German and Russian scientists, with cooks and doctors in attendance, horses to ride, and a military escort to ensure their safety; and it carried thousands of pounds' weight of preserved foods, tents, tools, and instruments on two hundred pack animals. These later travellers had every possible assistance from the Soviet Government and every conceivable luxury at their disposal on their way to make scientific researches in the Pamirs.

We need scarcely wonder that Rickmers reports that the Qirghiz demanded the most exorbitant prices for provisions supplied and specimens collected. He draws therefrom the false conclusion that the vaunted Qirghiz hospitality is dead. I refuse to believe that the few years which had elapsed between my journey and Rickmers' could have produced so radical a change in the century-old traditions of the nomads. It is more reasonable to assume that the obvious wealth of so well-equipped an expedition, and the presence of soldiers of the hated Red Army, provoked the phenomenon. I myself lived for months on the generous hospitality of the Qirghiz, and I can recall only a few negligible cases in which payment or services were asked from me in return. Such instances occurred only with people who had been to Samarqand, Bukhara, Tashkent, or Skobeleff and who had brought back with them the chaffering spirit of the town.

If I describe the daily life of one of these *auls* I describe them all, for their ways are uniform. According to their own standards the Qara Qirghiz are immensely rich. The 300,000 or so who inhabit the Alai regions own between them some 70,000 camels, a million horses, about half a million cows and yaks, and a good ten million sheep. Want and anxiety are as remote from them as drink and gambling. They neither smoke opium like the Bukharans nor *charas* like the Tajiks. The only passions they indulge in are games on horseback and eating the root of the gulchem. Gulchem root tastes and smells like rotting garlic. With practice and goodwill Europeans can get used to it. Rice and bread are both rare in the Alai. The Qirghiz occasionally barter sheep and wool for them with the dwellers in the lower valleys. But they are always reluctant to part with their sheep, so in the main they content themselves with gulchem root, which they dry, pound into flour, and use for the flat cakes which are their substitute for bread.

In summer the men go off to hunt with their hawks and eagles, or shoot the nimble ibex with the ancient muzzle-loading matchlock on its forked rest. The ibex is almost extinct in Europe but still exists wild in great numbers in the Alai. I usually accompanied the Qirghiz on these hunting expeditions. With two days' supply of food the hunter climbs up into the steep ravines and proceeds first to observe the game's usual haunts and habits. When he has assured himself of these he props his gun on its rest, presents it, keeps the match ready for lighting, and when all is thus in order no power on earth will induce him to quit his post until the ibex crosses his line of fire – which may not be for days. There then resounds a report like that of a small cannon, which echoes a thousandfold amongst the rocks with the most appalling din. I never saw an ibex get away. Every shot was a bull's-eye.

People in Europe are frequently under the impression that the Qirghiz and other nomadic races roam from one place to another in pure wilfulness. This is of course sheer nonsense. They are compelled to change their pastures to preserve their cattle and themselves. Their large herds need immense spaces for grazing. Climatic conditions and the nature of the Turkistan terrain compel them to shift their camps. In the autumn they move down to the warmest and most southerly parts of their territory, while in spring as the snows retreat they gradually return to the high-lying plateaux.

Each Qirghiz family has its own definite section of pasture, and its rights therein are scrupulously respected by other families and tribes, so that quarrels about grazing rights are almost unheard of.

In the Amu Darya regions I had often had opportunity to observe Qirghiz hunting gazelle with eagles. The moment a herd of these incredibly fleet deer are disturbed they take to flight, with the Qirghiz, on their swiftest horses, at their heels. The eagle is perched on its owner's arm. At the right moment he snatches off its hood and flings the bird from him. Swift as an arrow the eagle overtakes the gazelles, swoops on its victim, and pecks out its eyes. The wretched deer falls to the ground blinded and in agony, and is whisked into the saddle by the galloping hunter, and borne home in triumph to his yurt.

Once in Burdalik I was able to watch how the Qirghiz train their hunting eagles. The heads of freshly slaughtered sheep were set up on poles and the Qirghiz taught the young eagles to go at once for the eye-sockets, which were filled with red chunks of raw meat continually renewed.

One day the *aul* suddenly throbbed with excitement. A troup of wandering entertainers had arrived – *kumancha*-players, dancers, and a story-teller. These people travel from camp to camp to cater for the nomads' amusement. That evening a great fire was lit beside the *aqsaqal*'s tent. Carpets and felt rugs were spread round, boiling water for tea hissed in numberless kettles on their tripods, and the *chilim* circulated from mouth to mouth. The story-teller sat down near the fire and began to recite his tales in a monotonous voice. Though the listeners might have heard his stories a hundred times before, they never failed to thrill to them afresh. Every eye watched the old man's toothless mouth and not a sound was to be heard save his voice and the crackling of burning juniper.

'O you brave heroes! O you rich owners of great herds! O you tamers of the bear! I will tell you the story of the lovely Princess Neppez. High up in the Pamirs, near the Lake of Qara'ul, there once dwelt a Qirghiz prince, Saghur Khan, whose riches and whose cruelty were notorious throughout the whole of Turkistan. Beside every river, beside every glacier, beside every field of snow, the Khan posted his watchmen and allowed no one to draw water who had not first paid his tax into the Khan's fort. The price of the water was a maiden. Soon the people had no girl children left to pay their water-tax, and the Khan then demanded from them skins and furs instead. When these had likewise been exhausted, he demanded sheep and camels, so that in a few years the Qirghiz of the Roof of the World were reduced to poverty and suffered untold hunger. One day Princess Neppez, the daughter of Saghur Khan, rode out to hunt. Before long she spied an arghali sheep and threw her spear. She hastened up to draw the spear from the wound, when, lo, a wonderfully handsome youth lay at her feet, with whom she promptly fell in love. A few days later some poor Qirghiz stood once more before the Khan and begged for the grant of a little water. The princess was present and saw that her beloved was amongst the petitioners. The Khan set his warriors on to drive the hapless Qirghiz off with whips, but the princess placed herself in front of her lover to protect him, so that the warriors did not dare to touch him. When the Khan saw this, he flung the youth and his daughter both into a dungeon. When night fell the youth took Neppez by the hand, the wall opened like a door before him, and he led the princess out. He then confessed to her that he was the son of the mighty magician Baha ud Din and had been sent forth by his father to help the Qirghiz against the cruel Khan. Thereupon he uttered an all-prevailing curse and the Khan's castle with its owner sank into the waters of the Qara'ul. And since that day, the waters of the Pamirs are free to all.'

The men sat on in entranced silence. The narrator reached out for a *chilim* and slowly blew the smoke through his nostrils with enjoyment. This roused the Qirghiz to wild applause, for they do not know this method of smoking. After he had drunk a few basins of tea enriched with salt and fat, he began again.

'Do you know the story of Abdullah Bezdik? Nay, you cannot know it, for Allah revealed it to me in a dream. Listen, brave men! In the days of Tamerlane there lived at the court of Samarqand a certain mirza [scribe] called Abdullah Bezdik. The mirza had a great love of animals and could not bear to see them suffer. He used to go round the caravanserais of Samarqand and buy up every camel that he saw come in sick or wounded from its journeyings. One day the great Tamerlane heard of the mirza's doings and sent for him. Tamerlane was seated on a throne with a circle of many imams and mullas round him, when the mirza came in and prostrated himself again and again before the mighty Ruler of the World. Then Tamerlane asked why in the name of Allah he bought up a lot of sick camels which, after all, had no souls and were worth even less than so many women. The mirza answered that animals also had souls and suffered pain. The imams and mullas blenched at such blasphemy and challenged the mirza to prove that the camel had a soul. If he could not prove it he must die. The mirza replied that he could not prove it, since it was not possible to prove that even men had souls.

'Tamerlane was still more enraged at this reply and bade them strike off the impudent fellow's head. Before this order could be carried out the Court Fool interposed:

' "Tell me, mighty Timur, had the late Diwan Begi a soul or not?"

' "By Allah," cried Tamerlane, "I shall execute any man that doubts it!"

' "And shall you let the mirza go free if I prove that camels have a soul?" asked the Fool.

' "By the beard of the Prophet, I promise to let him go free. But how wilt thou prove it, Fool?"

' "Right easily, thou favourite of Allah! Thou hast just now

109

declared that the Diwan Begi had a soul, and how often, oh my Master, hast thou not thyself called him a camel!"

'Tamerlane, the imams, and the mullas laughed till the roof threatened to fall in. But the mirza was free.'

The story-teller was rewarded by loud applause and hearty laughter, such as only the children of nature know. When the *chilim* had gone the rounds again, he resumed:

'Now I shall tell you the story of Muqanna, the Veiled Prophet of Khorasan. Once upon a time he was obliged to fly from Merv to Bukhara, and there he built himself a fortress so strong that not a hundred thousand enemies could take it. He withdrew into his fortress with his five hundred wives and a young Negro slave. None but the women and the slave ever saw his face. One day many thousands of the Faithful gathered before the fort and begged Muqanna to withdraw the veil from his countenance. The Prophet sent them a message that if he were to grant their request they would all be shattered by the sight of his glory and would surely die. But the Faithful had no fear, and vowed that death would be sweet in the light of the Prophet's countenance.

'Thereupon the Prophet announced to them that he would show himself in the gate of the fortress towards the going down of the sun. They should await him there. When the rays of the setting sun were falling direct on the gate of the fortress the Prophet stationed in the court his five hundred wives with mirrors in their hands. Then the gate was flung open. The rays of the sun flashed from hundreds of mirrors and blinded the Faithful so that they fell to earth in terror. When the gates were closed again the worshippers of Muqanna remained many days in prayer before the fortress and glorified the irresistible radiance of the Prophet.'

The story-teller made a pause, and it was remarkable with what deep emotion his hearers listened after all these centuries to everything that had to do with the fate of the Prophet Muqanna. Presently the old man went on:

'The whole world hearkened to the teaching of Muqanna and was subject to him. Only the Prince Saiyid i Hirzi of Arabia was rebellious and threatened to make war. With innumerable warriors and slaves he advanced on Bukhara and besieged the fortress of the Prophet. The warriors of Saiyid i Hirzi had already conquered the town and the outer works of the fort; only that part of it which Muqanna himself defended still held out, proof against all attack. The Prophet's friends had fled from him in terror, when they saw that defeat was inevitable, and Muqanna stood face to face with death. He would not, however, fall living into the hands of his enemies lest they should look upon his face, which no mortal eye had ever seen. He prepared a final banquet for his wives and poured poison into the wine. All drank of it. One wife alone had observed the Prophet as he poured the poison; she tipped her draught into the bosom of her dress, but feigned to die. This woman later told Saiyid i Hirzi what had occurred.

'Muqanna had had a large oven heated for three long days and into it he dragged all his treasures. Then he smote the head off his one male slave and with the young man's body in his arms he leaped into the flames and was consumed with all his riches. For days Saiyid i Hirzi kept watch before the glowing oven for the reappearance of Muqanna, but he was never seen again.

'When Allah then sent the True Prophet Muhammad to earth his first command to all Believers was to abstain from wine, which had caused the downfall of Muqanna.'

The old man went on story-telling for hours, till I was weary and lay down to sleep. But for a long time after I could still hear his voice, and next morning the *aqsaqal* told me that the sun had risen before the last tale was told.

If only time had not been pressing, I should have loved to stay longer amongst these magnificent and delightful people. As it was, I had lingered rather too long everywhere and I was getting afraid that the Pamir passes would be too deeply under snow to let me cross. When the time came to say farewell I was liberally supplied with provisions for the road, and when I started off half the tribe accompanied me the first part of the way.

For days I marched steadily eastwards along the age-old, now half-forgotten caravan route that links Bukhara with Kashgar and China. The valley grew narrower, the cliffs alongside grew steeper. Bushes of camel thorn and stumps of artemisia furnished fuel for my camp fire. As long as the weather was good I was glad to bivouac in the open, on the banks of the Qizil Su or one of the numberless small tributaries which flow down, more particularly from the side of the Trans-Alai. The ground was thickly populated with marmots. Wherever I turned, there they were, each like a sentinel at the mouth of his burrow, upright as if to beg, and diving like lightning out of sight, with a sharp whistle, the moment I came into view.

Ruined and crumbling mud houses, graves adorned with horse-tails and ibex horns, little tumble-down mosques, and uncounted animal skeletons bore witness to the fact that this road had once been one of the most important arteries of Asia. Seven hundred and twelve years ago Kuchluk, the Emperor of Qara Khotan, fled through this valley with Jebe, general of Chingiz Khan, hot in pursuit. Jebe overtook him at Daraut Qurghan, struck his head off, and brought it in triumph to Chingiz Khan, who mounted it in silver and used it to decorate his throne in camp by the Kerulen River.

For days past the summits of the Trans-Alai had been swathed in mist and the nights were growing colder. I had distinctly taken too long in coming and now anxiously determined to push on to Sari Tash as quickly as possible, hoping that I might be in time to get over the Taldik Pass to Osh before the heavier snows began to fall.

I ought easily to have managed the sixty-five miles from Daraut Qurghan to Sari Tash in three days. By dawdling in the Qirghiz *auls* I had taken nearly a fortnight to cover the one short stretch. When I got to Sari Tash I found a caravan halting there which had come from Gulcha, and had been overtaken by a snowstorm on the Taldik, from which they had escaped with the utmost difficulty. Despite their haste and care, sixteen of their animals had died in the storm. The leader of the caravan assured me that no further crossing of the Taldik would now be possible until the spring.

Fate had banged the door in my face. The caravan was to start next day for Daraut Qurghan, whither it was bound. I summoned up all my wisdom and philosophy and decided to turn and go back with it.

X

On the Roof of the World

Some hundreds of camels tinkled their bells merrily in the early morning air, and my donkeys were already loaded up waiting for the start, when a lively hullabaloo was heard in the bullet-riddled rest-house. I went along to see what was happening. A horde of Qirghiz had just arrived, and, as far as I could descry in the grey light of a bitter morning, hundreds of laden camels were passing by us, taking the road to the Pamirs.

A number of the new-comers were standing in a group with our caravan-*bashi*, amongst them the *aqsaqal* of the *aul* where I had spent my last six days. From him I learnt that my Qirghiz friends were in flight from detachments of the Tajik Red Army and some Soviet officials who had come into the Alai Valley to take a census of the nomads in their winter quarters. The Qirghiz didn't need to be told that such a census would be accompanied by a registration of their names and tribes, and would ultimately be followed by the imposition of taxes. Thousands of yurts were hastily struck, and the nomads were now retracing their steps to their summer grazing grounds round the Qara Kul, choosing rather to defy the horrors of winter in the heights than let themselves be helplessly put through their paces by the Soviet officials. When the *aqsaqal* in all seriousness invited me to accompany them and spend the winter with them amongst the snows of the high Pamirs I jumped at the offer. Without taking further time for reflection I drove my donkeys off to join their caravan and fell in myself.

If the mountain-bred Qirghiz were prepared to face the Pamir winter why should I funk it? Where such a multitude proposed to

114

The Qirghiz in flight to the Pamirs

live themselves, they would not let their guest and protégé perish in their midst. When I asked the *aqsaqal* whether his tribal brethren would not raise objections to feeding a feringi free for months at a time – for I wasn't in a position to pay very much – he laughed and promised that I should be his guest.

The *aqsaqal* and his companions stayed by the nearest tents till the whole tribe had passed through. The welter of men and animals forcibly reminded me of scenes during the World War. Long lines of camels and yaks, piled high with loads, passed by; armed men dashed hither and thither amongst them, brandishing whips and urging them to greater speed. Not a soul was left in the valley save the herdsmen in charge of the herds; every other living thing on legs was up and away. Other tribes and families from the many side valleys of the Alai had likewise taken fright and were off to the mountains too. They thrust themselves amongst our people and increased the confusion of the throng. I was surprised to see the enormous stores of fodder that were being brought along, and when I inquired about it the *aqsaqal* informed me that they had known for months that the Soviets had designs on their freedom and they had therefore taken time by the forelock and set about accumulating large stores of food for their yaks and camels.

The sheep, cows, and horses had to be left behind because it would not have been possible to carry off enough to feed them through the whole long winter. Several thousand sheep accompanied our march, however; they were to be slaughtered at the Qara Kul and frozen for our winter meat supply. At last the peoples of the Qazaq had all passed by and we joined the train. The sun had now risen and I looked back down the valley. To an enormous distance I could see camel train after camel train; the entire horde was on trek, flying from the officials of the Soviets. The news of the Russian approach must have spread like a forest fire, and by the time the officials reached the grazing grounds they found the land empty save for the herdsmen, who, when questioned as to the whereabouts of the owners of the herds, just shook their heads and answered: 'Far away! Far away!'

After an hour of climbing up a height we had to descend again to wade across the Qizil Su. The animals had to be led one by one, and with the greatest caution, through the raging water at the one fordable spot. With such multitudes to be handled this caused great delay, and it was almost night before we were able to pitch a hastily devised camp at the resting-place of Bur Tapa, at a height of about 11,400 feet. There could be no question of erecting the yurts. After the animals had been attended to, each man wrapped himself in his felt blankets and rolled over close to some of the animals to share their warmth. We were to start early. I lay long awake, breathing the pure mountain air with delight, and listening to the howling of the wolves which prowled round the camp, till the murmuring of the Bur Tapa torrent which flows down from the glaciers of the Qizil Aghin eventually lulled me to sleep. The whistling and howling of the dreaded Pamir wind woke me early, so that I was up and about by the time the Qirghiz began to load up.

Our road that day led us through narrow gorges and steeply upwards over innumerable zigzag tracks. We crossed the Qizil Art Pass at some 13,700 feet and found it deep in snow. At night we pitched a hasty camp, like that of yesterday, at the station of Kok Sai. Behind this pass, almost at the height of the summit of Mont Blanc, there stands a cairn. Some poles with horse-tail banners and numerous arghali horns proclaim the fact that a Qirghiz saint lies buried here, whose name is said to have been Qizil Art. The caravans make a practice of halting at this spot to offer prayers of thanksgiving that they have safely reached the Roof of the World.

The night at this height was bitterly cold, and by the morning mountain sickness had me in a powerful grip. I had the greatest difficulty in keeping my seat on the camel I had been lent, and was repeatedly sick. Though I filled my nostrils with snow according to the best advice I could not stem the tide of blood. Just in sight of the Qizil Kul I had so severe an attack of vertigo that I fell off my camel, fortunately without seriously hurting myself, for the soft snow received me gently. The Qirghiz packed me into a rude litter made of the poles of a yurt and tied me safely into it. When I began

117

to feel a little better I stuck my head out and looked round. After we had crossed the Uit Bulaq pass, the almost inky waters of the Qara Kul could be seen somewhat below us in the distance, with icebergs over three feet high floating on the surface. At Qara Kul we pitched our last camp but one. I still felt sick, and could not bear even the sight of food. The Qirghiz were much distressed, and kept plying me with hot tea, for which the *aqsaqal* nobly sacrificed great chunks of a sugar-loaf, since I energetically refused the ingredients of salt and mutton fat.

The farther we descended the more overwhelming was the immense view in every direction over the gigantic plateau in which the Qara Kul lake is situated. In the triangle formed by the two streams the Qizil Jik and the Aq Shilga we finally pitched the permanent camp, which, as it proved, was to be my home for seven months to come. At my request a separate yurt was set up for me, which I intended to make as cosy and comfortable as circumstances would permit. The Qirghiz made very merry over me when I tried to help the women to erect the felt tents. Mahmud Sharaieff, my friend the *aqsaqal*, disapprovingly explained to me that setting up the yurts was woman's work and unbecoming for a man. Where-upon I sat me down upon the ground nearby and watched the women with the dignity seemly in a man.

The yurt is unquestionably one of the greatest inventions Asia has brought forth. Its circular structure and dome-like roof combine the maximum of comfort with extraordinary stability. During my stay on the Pamirs the heaviest storms raged over the *aul* without a moment's cessation all through January, yet never once was even one yurt blown down. The skeleton of the yurt consists of strong wooden poles from five-eighths to an inch thick, which are lashed together with thin thongs. These form the side walls. On top of these, bent poles are attached which are lashed to a circular hoop about the size of a cart wheel. This central ring, which forms the top of the tent, serves both as ventilator and chimney. The average height of a yurt is about eight to ten feet, and its inner diameter about twenty-six feet. The walls and roof are covered on the outside with thick felts, which are made fast with cords tied firmly round. The inner wall of the tent is also clothed with felt, stamped with simple coloured designs. The inner wall may be further covered with gaily coloured carpets, which have achieved world fame under the collective name of Samarqand carpets. The reason of this is, no doubt, that even before the Great War wily traders used to buy them up from the nomads and export them from

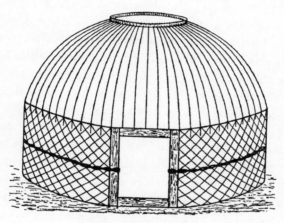

Diagram of a Qirghiz Yurt

Samarqand. The floor of the yurt is spread with thin felt in summer. In winter, however, they first lay a thick layer of felt on the bare ground, over this a layer of dried grass or dung three or four inches deep, with another layer of felt rugs on top. Even when the temperature is at its lowest this padded floor prevents any feeling of chill. In the centre of the yurt a round space is left free for the fireplace. In the valleys this is where the charcoal-burning *manqal* stands, but in the mountains, where charcoal is unprocurable, a fire built with the cakes of dried cattle dung smoulders here day and night. The door consists simply of a wooden frame; in the summer it stands open, but in the winter the opening is screened with a multiple curtain of felt rugs and carpets.

After living for many months in the yurts of the Qirghiz I fully shared their dislike of the usual mud huts affected by the settled populations. These mud buildings are cold in winter and in summer exposed to invasions of every imaginable kind of vermin, while in the yurts I never saw vermin of any kind, with the exception of lice, nor any scorpions or tarantulas. The Qirghiz maintain that neither the giant spider nor the scorpion will venture to set foot on felt.

My host, the *aqsaqal*, placed two young Qirghiz girls at my disposal, to serve me. While I rolled about on my bedding of felt blankets, still in the grip of mountain sickness, they sat by the fire and sewed me a wonderful coat of ibex skins, and a warm fur cloak of innumerable marmot skins, to protect me against the cold. Every day at sunrise the womenfolk went out with camels and collected for firewood stunted bushes of such kinds as grew, sparsely enough, in the neighbourhood of the camp and round the lake. Soon whole mountains of fuel were stacked between the yurts, skilfully placed to enjoy either the shelter of the yurts themselves or else the lee of some cliff, so that they could not be carried off by the storms.

After three weeks of illness I was at last well enough to come out of my yurt. I had unfortunately no thermometer to gauge the prevailing temperatures, so that I could only guess at them. The nearer we came to November the colder it grew. Soon the fire in the yurt had to be kept burning continuously by day as well as by night, and nevertheless water and milk were permanently frozen. As long as the weather was in any degree tolerable the men went off to hunt, and I with them.

The whole mountain basin in which the lake lay seemed dead and oddly unreal. All cliff and rock faces are rounded off, glazed and polished by the perpetual wind and sandstorms. Fine, yellow sand fills every crack and cranny in the rocks, so that the whole landscape looks as if it had been varnished over with a solution of melted yellow glass. The great Qara Kul lake is about seventy-five or eighty square miles in area, and its banks carry out the same scheme of decoration, for they are edged with shining yellow boulders. The only vegetation occurs where the snouts of great glaciers push their tongues out nearly to the lake and form great marshes in which a few species of mountain plant are able to flourish. All round the lake the ground is strewn with skeletons of camels and horses which have either starved to death or been devoured by wolves.

Every day we bagged numbers of ibex, wild mountain sheep, and marmots. Our hunting expeditions often lasted several days and my companions and I rode off towards the south in the direction of the Indian frontiers, as far as the source of the Amu Darya, which cuts its way westward through wild, romantic, and untrodden valleys.

While we were busy hunting, the women in the camp looked after the children, milked the camels and donkeys, made clothing, and collected dung for fuel. When we were at home I used to have to turn the two girls out of my yurt every night, for they showed signs of intending to settle down in it for good.

One day Fate, in the form of the *aqsaqal*, approached me. He came into my yurt one evening, sat down by the fire, and began to take long draughts of the tea I offered him. Then he let fly:

'You are no longer a stranger and an *urus* in our *aul*!' I guessed what the wily old man was trying to get at, and as I had long foreseen some such proposition I had an answer ready:

'You speak truly, O my father.'

'At home in your own country have you a lady wife who waits on you?'

Manfully I lied: 'Yes, my father.'

'It isn't right that you should live alone in your yurt. The days are short and the nights are long. Your lady will understand if you take a servant girl to bed.'

'In my country that isn't done, father. Besides I am poor. I have neither camel nor horse to offer as a bride-price.'

'No one will think of expecting a bride-price from you. The bigger girl who is serving you has no relations but a grandmother. She is willing to let you take the girl for nothing. I have talked the matter over with her.'

'I'll think about it, father.'

'You have hunted the ibex with us, and the marmot. You eat our sheep and drink our tea. No *urus* has ever lived amongst us as you do. We all like you and we well understand that you cannot stay with us forever, but the girls weep and want to live in your tent with you.'

'But I should rather live alone and do my own work myself.'

I had said all this loudly and positively, which was a grave breach of Qirghiz etiquette, for serious matters between men are always discussed in a quiet undertone.

'The men will laugh at you.'

'I'll think about it and give you my answer in a few days. I must first talk the matter over with my God.'

The old man lifted the corner of a carpet and spat forcibly underneath, which meant that he thought me a hopeless and benighted idiot.

A miss is as good as a mile. One reason for my refusal was that I was afraid of infection, for all the dwellers in Central Asia are riddled with venereal disease. Moreover, the Qirghiz womenfolk hardly come up to our standards either of beauty or cleanliness. I often used to watch them sitting in the sun obligingly picking the lice out of each other's hair and popping them into their mouths with manifest enjoyment. This filled me with such uncontrollable disgust that I should gladly have banished them from my yurt even by day.

For a few days I was left in peace, then the *aqsaqal* paid me another call. Again he sat down by the fire, put salt and fat into his tea, and swallowed it with noisy grunts:

'I was a guest in your yurt the other day.'

'Indeed I remember, father.'

'I then spoke to you about Maimakha!'

'Yes, father.'

'Her grandmother says that Maimakha is fifteen and the girl says she will no longer be unwed, for she feels it is a disgrace.'

'She must marry another then.'

'But she wants to marry you, my brother.'

'Since when is it the custom amongst the Qirghiz that the girl should seek out for herself the man she wants to marry?'

For a long time the old man sat silent, staring into the fire.

'Take a whip and thrash the idea out of her head. Thus you will have peace.'

'You forget, my father, that I am, after all, an *urus*. In my country no man strikes a woman.'

Another lengthy pause. I filled the *chilim* with Farghana tobacco and held it towards my guest. Then I gave tongue again to make an end of the business.

'Father, do you know what a *kafir* is?'

'Yes, an Unbeliever.'

'Well, look you, I am an Unbeliever, and moreover I am a penitent and I have taken on me a vow not for three years to touch a woman. Am I to break my vow for Maimakha's sake? That you could not ask of me.'

Shaking his head, the old man stood up, wrapped his fur mantle about him, and went out. After that evening I heard no more of marriage and a few weeks later I learned that Maimakha had consoled herself and was going to be married in a few days, not to a poor penniless devil like me, but to a fine young Qirghiz, who was able to pay a handsome bride-price for her.

Preparations for the forthcoming festivity were eagerly begun. The women brewed *buzah*, a drink with a revolting taste and smell, made from *qumiz*. It is extremely intoxicating and is only used on festive occasions, for the Qirghiz are normally very temperate.

Two large cast-iron pots are set up and their mouths covered with fresh, still-bleeding sheepskins. As these dry they shrink, and cling tightly to the pot, sealing it almost hermetically. As a further precaution they are then sealed with wet mud. A round hole is then made in the centre of each sheepskin cover, and the two vessels are connected with each other by a tube. The larger had been filled almost to the brim with *qumiz*. A large fire was now made under this one, and the steam from it passed into the second, where it condensed into a thick milky fluid with a high alcohol content. *Buzah* possesses the doubtful advantage of intoxicating you twice over. When the Qirghiz had slept off their first orgy on the day after the wedding, they drank water. A few minutes later they were staggering about thoroughly drunk again. This curious result seems to be caused by the fact that some of the thick fluid remains in the stomach, and when more water is supplied releases a second dose of alcohol.

To initiate the feast, as it were, on the morning of the wedding day three hundred riders took part in a *baigha*. And here I had the opportunity to observe that the Qirghiz are, if possible, better riders and better stayers than the Turkomans. With the wildest cries and shouts they galloped up and down the steepest gradients and fell off in masses, so that I pictured myself having dozens of broken arms and legs to set. But, except for a few bruises, not a soul was hurt. Songs followed, accompanied by monotonous music coaxed by their owners from some primitive guitars and violins. After this the bride-price, consisting of two camels and two yaks, was solemnly presented to Maimakha's grandmother. This was the signal for a general orgy of *buzah* drinking, and within an hour there was not a single sober person in the camp except myself. The ghastly sour taste of the stuff had prevented my doing justice to my opportunities. I was chaffed on all sides for having refused the lovely bride – who was proudly wearing her towering bridal head-dress for all to see – when I might have had her for nothing! The bridegroom did not seem to mind in the least that a stupid feringi had turned his nose up at the beautiful bride. I asked whether Maimakha had entered matrimony as a virgin. They told me that no one would expect this of a girl of fifteen. While men and women alike lay strewn about the camp completely drunk, the new-made husband took his bride by the hand and drew the tottering girl into his yurt. That completed the one and only marriage ceremony.

A penniless Qirghiz cannot hope to find a wife and set up an independent establishment of his own. He must first raise the necessary bride-price. In such a case the youth either hires himself out to a fellow tribesman as a herd-boy and saves until he has acquired the necessary animals, or thieves them from other tribes. If a husband dies, the widow has not the right to return to her own parents or to look round for another husband; she is inherited by the surviving relatives in precisely the same way as her husband's tents and herds. Whether she thus becomes the property of her husband's father or brother, she serves her new owner to the end of her days as beast of burden or as concubine, just as he happens to prefer. The Qirghiz have no incest inhibitions and near relatives are free to intermarry if they like.

Till the very last Maimakha had continued to work for me in my tent. After she was married I was left with only Belem, an ugly girl, but willing and extraordinarily hard-working. At the first streak of dawn every morning, as regular as clockwork, she turned up in my yurt, and disappeared in the evening when I indicated that I wanted to go to sleep. The mountain sickness had completely disappeared, and I felt as fit and happy as a fish in its home waters.

I had made myself candles of mutton fat with wicks of cotton. When such a storm was raging that even the hardy Qirghiz did not go out to hunt I would light some of these home-made candles for myself and with such primitive tools as were available I repaired every sort of household gear for the whole tribe; I tinkered up guns and revolvers, the locks of chests, and the buckles of straps; I soldered the holes in cooking vessels and mended *manqals*. At such times my yurt would be packed to its utmost capacity with men who had called in to watch me at my work. They looked on in amazement. One day I succeeded in making a trap for marmots; it proved successful and I made many more.

When the storm eased off a bit, I was tempted out to hunt ibex or to fish – unsuccessfully – in the lake. The Qara Kul appears to be completely innocent of fish; the only living thing in it is a minute type of crab, of which there are immense numbers. The Qirghiz told me that in summer large numbers of birds, whose names they did not know, come and nest by the lake, but they disappear again

125

in autumn. The lake was usually covered with a thin sheet of ice; when I broke this and tasted the water I noticed a faint trace of salt and saltpetre.

The months sped by. My standard of living had sunk to the same level as that of the Qirghiz. Eating, hunting, and sleeping were our watchwords, and I grew fat in the process. I ought to have been in Tabriz months ago. Qannadi had probably long since presumed that I had fallen a victim to my love of adventure, and I loved to picture the surprise that would greet my return. But that day was still far off. On Christmas Eve I had made eighteen tiny candles and fastened them on a small bush of camelthorn inside my yurt. Then I expended my last stores of rice and sugar in cooking a festive dish and invited in my best friends. My illuminated tree evoked general amazement and delight, and hearty grief was expressed that the shares of rice were so small, for my pudding was much appreciated. To celebrate the occasion I had unearthed my razor and my guests scarcely recognised me without my magnificent full beard.

At the beginning of March, light showers of snow began to fall and the whole scene was transformed into a wonderful polar landscape. Rock walls and stone shoots and the frozen lake itself were all covered deep in snow. Exactly opposite the entrance to my tent the Ushba glacier thrust downward almost to our camp, whilst in the west the far-flung ice-fields of the Tanima massif gleamed in the sun. It grew warmer with the coming of the snow, and the wind-storms became less frequent and severe.

Before long the skin was hanging in tatters from every exposed part of my body, and even thick layers of mutton fat could only partially protect it from the ravages of the fierce sun.

Thus passed March and April. At the beginning of May the snow disappeared as quickly as it had come, and within a few days young green was sprouting between the stones, though it is true it was so scanty that I could rejoice over every individual plantling that I found.

Towards the middle of May the camp began to break up. The

Qirghiz were off to the valley of the Qizil Su, and thence eastwards into Chinese territory, while I intended to follow the Qizil Su downstream to the Amu Darya. A few camel-riders went off in advance, to conduct the huge herds out of the Alai valley to the rendezvous at Sari Tash.

By the 24th of May all was ready for the start. Every one was in the highest spirits. Even the half-starved animals seemed to understand that they were bound at last for luscious meadows, and contentedly let themselves be loaded up, however heavily. Two days later we halted in the valley of the Qizil Su, by the ruins of the Sari Tash *rabat*. Much more snow was lying here than we had left behind us nearly 5,000 feet higher up, and it had to be shovelled away before the yurts could be set up. Before I said farewell to my Qirghiz friends I hastily exchanged my two donkeys for a good camel, and when the actual moment of parting came the whole tribe accompanied me for several hours on my way.

At Ursham I met the herds coming up the valley. For hours a broad river of sheep, cows, and horses flowed past me, carefully shepherded by men and dogs. Then these were gone and I was saying a last good-bye to the son of the *aqsaqal*, who was acting as rear-guard to the procession. Hot tears suddenly filled my eyes, though I little suspected at the time that I had been the witness of the last march of the free Qirghiz.

About eighteen or nineteen miles farther west a large body of mounted men suddenly appeared in front of me. They were instantly recognisable as military, and were accompanied by camels and mules carrying supplies. I and my baggage were subjected to a minute examination. They listened with incredulity to my hastily improvised lie that I had spent the whole winter alone in Sari Tash. I gradually discovered the purpose of their march. They had come from Dushamba, the capital of Tajikistan, and were to effect a junction at Sari Tash with a military column coming from Farghana via Osh. The combined force was then going to push on to Pamirski Post to give the *coup de grace* to the robbers and rebels of the neighbourhood. This detachment was equipped as if it were starting out to besiege a mighty fortress rather than a miserable little fort held by a handful of undisciplined highwaymen.

If once the Soviets succeeded in making a pukka base on the Pamirs, good-bye forever to the freedom of the Qirghiz nomads. Tempting taxes could be levied on the living wealth of the Qirghiz flocks and herds, and assuredly the enlightened government of the new Russia would not let so rich a source of revenue slip through its fingers. It would also endeavour to curb, if not entirely to suppress, the economic and political freedom of the last of all genuinely free peoples on earth, by incorporating them within the Union of the Soviets.

The Russian government of the tsars had twice attempted – but only twice – to impose its will on the nomad races of Turkistan, and had attempted it very gingerly, hoping by gradual stages to prepare the ground for a complete conquest. As a first step small castles and palaces were built at State expense for the more important tribal chiefs, in the hopes that the Qirghiz might thus be tempted to adopt a more settled form of life. The Khans, however, erected their yurts as usual round these handsome new buildings and lived as of old in their tents whenever they came into the neighbourhood. The new and princely buildings served conveniently as cattle stalls!

A second step, an attempt to get hold of the Qirghiz on the religious side, was no less abortive. The Russian government sent hundreds of Muhammadan mullas to the Qirghiz tribes – who were originally the purest pagans – under the illusion that all Asiatics were Muslims. The Qirghiz are devoted to story-tellers: they let the mullas talk away, and had not the least objection to adopting Islam – nominally – when the mullas proposed it. Almost all the tribes in future proclaimed themselves Muslims, but they allowed the mullas and the teachings of Islam not the slightest influence over them – which influence was of course what St. Petersburg had hoped to see established. After these futile efforts, the tsarist government left the Qirghiz in peace.

No such tolerance was of course to be expected from the Soviets. The Qirghiz had noted with dismay the fate that had overtaken the settled communities, and up till now they had contrived to guard their freedom in the almost inaccessible spaces of the Pamirs, for which reason they were assisted as far as possible by the rebels who

Detachment after detachment of the Red Army passed me, riding up to the Pamirs

had taken possession of the abandoned military posts of the tsarist government and dug themselves comfortably in. If these posts were to fall into Soviet hands the fate of the Qirghiz was sealed.

A curious chance had made me the witness of the last act of this drama – the passing of Qirghiz freedom in Turkistan. A few weeks later I heard in Dushamba that the advancing forces of the Soviets had found all the barracks and frontier posts, Pamirski Post amongst them, entirely deserted. The rebel garrisons must have cleared out into Chinese territory as soon as they realised that they could not hope to offer effective resistance to the consolidated power of Russia. Possibly they had also run out of supplies and ammunition.

I had arrived back in Daraut Qurghan. In olden days it had been the busiest and most important frontier and customs post between the province of Bukhara and Russian Turkistan, but nowadays, since the establishment of a customs union between the various Soviet republics, it had lost its former glory. When I arrived I found a large military encampment; the troops were under canvas, acting as a reserve for the forces which had advanced up into the Pamirs.

My European clothes had long since fallen off me in tatters, and been exchanged for Qirghiz kit. Daraut Qurghan lies about 6,500 feet below the Qizil Art Pass, and this difference in altitude was forcibly emphasised by the heat of the sun. The slightest exertion set the sweat rolling down my body in streams beneath my Qirghiz furs. There was nothing for it but to barter my ibex skins for a Tajik robe and my heavy fur cap for a skull-cap and turban. I couldn't find a suitable pair of leather stockings such as the Sarts affect, so I was reduced to buying a pair of camel-hair ones. These are knotted like the carpets, and are extraordinarily hard-wearing.

The Alai valley narrows after you leave Daraut Qurghan. Woods and every kind of flowering bush rejoice the eye. Habitations grow more frequent and you soon meet green-clad, cultivated fields which indicate that you are reaching more populous regions. Passing through Kurg Su, Sau Ur, Sari Kul, Aji Khalma, and Aq Sai, I reached Damburchi at the junction of the Qizil Su and the Muk Su, which flows down from the glaciers of the Tanima. The augmented Qizil Su changes its name from henceforward to the Surkh Ab.

I saw but few nomad yurts in this neighbourhood, for all the Qirghiz families who could, had taken flight before the advance of the Red Army. Only Tajiks and Sarts had stood their ground. Rest-houses and *chai-khanas* became more frequent, and after nine months' deprivation I once more ate my fill of *shishlik* and was able to lay in a store of sugar and brick tea. I joyfully welcomed the sight

130

of cigarettes, for all this while I had been driven to console myself with the *chilim*.

After the Muk Su, the mountain country of the Qara Tegin (the Black Mountains) begins – one of the most dread regions of eastern Bukhara. Junipers become rarer, and everywhere there are clumps of silver poplar and black elm. There was no longer any point in living like a savage. I washed and shaved regularly – to the recurrent amusement of the villagers. They were tickled to death to see me soap myself and scratch the stubble off my cheeks with a small machine. The peoples of Turkistan never soap before shaving; they simply wet their beard with water and scrape it off. Any form of washing, except the prescribed religious ablutions – which they reduce to rinsing finger-tips and mouth – is absolutely unheard of.

After Damburchi the valley of the Surkh Ab widens out. The river is swollen by innumerable torrents which pour down from the snouts of the glaciers of the Peter the Great range. They roar through narrow gorges in frequent waterfalls, and tumble into the valley. Before reaching Yarai, I fell in with a lot of mountain Tajiks who were making their way on foot over the Dengiz Bai to Farghana. Many of them recognised me and stopped a moment to chat. They were folk whom I had met last autumn in the rest-house below the pass, when they were travelling in the opposite direction towards the Qara Tegin. Some of them were carrying loads but little lighter than those put on a donkey, yet these men were making twenty-two to twenty-five miles a day steadily uphill.

Yarai itself is a large village inhabited by Uzbegs and Tajiks. Rich orchards were standing in all the glory of white and rose-pink blossom. For months and months I had looked on nothing but red rocks, snow, and the mud-brown walls of nomad yurts, and the mud village of Yarai seemed by contrast a very paradise. Millions of wild roses were in flower and the meadows were pied with blue auriculas. In contrast to the Qirghiz, the Uzbeg and Tajik men work in the fields themselves, and their women folk are rarely seen by the passing stranger. The *ariqs* or small irrigation channels were being put in order everywhere, men were mowing the fields of tall clover, and magnificent dragon-flies, which are particularly abundant in this part of Bukhara, were darting about in their thousands. Despite the proximity of the capital, Bolshevik propaganda has so far made little progress in these parts. I scarcely saw an unveiled woman anywhere.

When I was spending the night in Langarash I was wakened early by the *chai-khana-chik* and ordered to leave his house. On my asking the reason, he informed me that this was Friday – the Muslim equivalent of Sunday – and the *aqsaqal* of the village did not allow an Unbeliever to spend Friday in the place. I asked the way to the *aqsaqal*'s house and protested against being turned out. It appeared that the mulla had persuaded him that some disaster would overtake the village if I were allowed to stay. I made no attempt at resistance, loaded up my camel, and set out for Garm.

The Surkh Ab at this point flows broad and powerful, forming in its course many islands, which are the home of every kind of waterfowl. The marked piety of the inhabitants of this neighbourhood is lucidated by the fact that even the tiniest village boasts its mosque. In contrast to the rest of Turkistan, the mosques are here built not of mud but of handsomely wrought timber, and the supporting pillars are skilfully carved and painted. The accompanying minarets are built clear of the mosque and are likewise of timber or of stone.

On the hills at each side of the valley I saw numerous hollow caves in almost inaccessible spots several hundred yards above the bottom of the valley. They were all inhabited, so that some thousands of troglodytes must be at home here. I confess I could see neither rhyme nor reason in this cave-dwelling business, since there was ample room below for thousands of houses. When I reached Garm, however, I discovered that the cave-dwellers form a special Bukharan sect, which in olden days was persecuted by the orthodox Muslims and took refuge in the rock caves. Though complete religious toleration nowadays prevails, they still prefer to live in their cave-homes and climb down steep and dangerous tracks for every drop of water.

Although Garm was formerly the seat of a beg and the capital of the eastern province of the Qara Tegin, it is one of the dirtiest and most miserable holes I have ever seen, even in Central Asia. Tumble-down houses, lanes several feet deep in swampy mud, a miserable bazaar in which neither cigarettes nor dried fruit can be bought, a dirty windowless Government office, and a crowd of sulky inhabitants are the essential characteristics of this provincial capital.

The road on leads across numerous narrow bridges and climbs steeply up to Ab i Garm, a place which I had already visited in 1919. Not far from the town, securely hidden in an almost inaccessible bowl-shaped depression amongst the rocks, thirty-six Austrians had forged weapons in the interests of their country during the World War, for use against the 'Russians', as the Bukharans understood the term. In 1916 the Amir of Bukhara got into touch with the prisoners of war in Kata Qurgham, Samarqand, and Tashkent and enlisted some first-class craftsmen, most of them expert munition-makers, who with the assistance of Sarts and Bukharans escaped from the prison camps and were piloted by secret tracks first to Bukhara and then to Ab i Garm. Here they succeeded in establishing a regular arsenal able to manufacture rifle ammunition and cannon balls. They got their machines and material by the most roundabout routes, mostly through China and Afghanistan. Machine-guns and trench mortars reached Ab i Garm in detached parts and were assembled by the Austrians. When the Russians surprised Bukhara, the Amir, as well as his statesmen and generals, lost their heads completely and bolted by the shortest route into Afghanistan.

On the second day of my stay in Ab i Garm I borrowed a horse from the *chai-khana-chik* and rode out to the ruins of the arsenal. The commando in charge of explosives had done its work thoroughly. Not one stone remained upon another. The waterworks were a heap of ruins, between which there still lay parts of water-leads, dynamos, and transmitters in the wildest confusion. Nearby some Tajiks had built stone hovels for themselves out of the wreckage. I had the greatest difficulty in winning their confidence and coaxing them to tell me all about the final capture of the arsenal. According to their story, fourteen Austrians were still surviving; with six hundred men of the regular Bukharan Army and the anti-Soviet freelances who had taken refuge here, they put up a bitter and determined resistance against the advancing Russian forces. Their admirable supply of munitions and their superior weapons enabled them to hold out for four months against the badly equipped Russians. They were not even short of food supplies, for they were able to draw on the fertile valleys in their rear. When the Russians found that they were powerless to break down their defence they summoned to their assistance two aeroplanes from Tashkent, and with this reinforcement they at last succeeded in capturing the arsenal. The survivors of the garrison were cut down without quarter. By the irony of fate the chief credit for the conquest of the arsenal fell to the International Iron Brigade, a force composed mainly of Hungarian and Austrian ex-prisoners of war, so that here again Austria's sons murdered each other in the interest of foreigners.

I sat a long time on the ruins of the building where once upon a time I had myself set up the machines for minting gold and silver coins for the Amir of Bukhara, till the fanatical mullas and muftis called a halt to my activities. Machines, they preached, were the work of the devil and money produced by them must not be allowed to desecrate the sacred soil of Bukhara. They stirred up so much fanatic hate that I was compelled to fly by night over the frontier.[1]

After quitting Ab i Garm I left the Surkh Ab, which had so long been my companion, and riding along by the side of one of its tributaries I climbed the mountain heights on which Faizabad is situated, the largest town of eastern Bukhara, with some two

1 See my earlier book, *Pascholl, Plenny!*

134

thousand houses. This valley is usually rich in fruits, and the first cherries and apricots of the season were already ripe. I let myself go in greedy enjoyment of them. The plateaux and high valleys between the Hisar mountains and the Darwaz range are the most fertile of all Tajikistan. Here the cultivation of the silkworm begins, and the innumerable mulberry trees give the landscape a peculiar character of its own.

XI

Through Uzbegistan

A tributary of the Kafir Nihan rises near Faizabad and for a time the road follows its course, to twist and turn later in zigzags up the steep mountain sides to Kafir Nihan. This town lies in a wide and lofty mountain basin on a river of the same name. The first time I travelled to Ab i Garm I was able to see very little of the place, for while the Qush Begi, in whose company I was, was receiving the Beg and the chief men of the district, I had to remain hidden away in my tent. Kafir Nihan forms as it were an island in the Muslim sea of Bukhara, for it is – as indeed its name implies – inhabited by Unbelievers who immigrated some hundred years ago from Kafiristan in Afghan territory. Legend tells that the Kafirs are the last remnants of a once extensive Christian community in Central Asia. Thanks to their adaptability and unfanatical behaviour they were for the most part tolerated by the Muslims except for an occasional massacre. Unlike the Jews they were permitted to purchase land and to enjoy the same rights as Muslims. Kafir Nihan is a clean, well-cared-for place with extensive vineyards.

The road now runs through a broad, extremely fertile valley to Dushamba (now rechristened Stalinabad), the capital of Tajikistan, with a population of round about 30,000. Dushamba was the first place of any size I had come to since leaving Skobeleff. The town had certainly gained much since the authorities and the Council of Tajikistan have made it their official headquarters. Many buildings in European style have been erected, amongst them a very passable hotel intended only for the use of travelling commissars or Soviet delegations. With special permission from the local Soviet it may, however, be also opened to ordinary mortals. The town streets, which elsewhere throughout the whole of Turkistan are the terror of travellers, are here kept in good repair, and during my stay Russian engineers were actually busy installing a small electric plant to supply the town with light and power.

The bazaars of Dushamba are as well provided with every kind of Asiatic goods as they are innocent of European wares. When I made inquiries the Russian 'Political Adviser' of the Tajik Soviet assured me that in pursuance of the Five Year Plan the Turkistan bazaars would soon all be well stocked with the products of Russian industry. There was notably a lack of every kind of metal article, for the demand for metal can be only very partially supplied from local resources.

Riding through the bazaar I saw a dealer in birds of prey who trained and sold eagles, falcons, and buzzards for the chase.

The very day of my arrival in Dushamba I loaded my camel with two sackfuls of mineral specimens and made my way to the 'Tajsoff' (Soviet of Tajikistan) to deposit them there for official dispatch to Samarqand. I had hoped to acquire merit with the Soviet Government by my collection of stones. My mistake! Various officials first of all examined my papers for an unholy length of time, and then inquired how I had managed to arrive in Tajikistan without the express permission of the Tajik Soviet. I explained that the authorities in Samarqand had given me plenary powers to make mineralogical researches in the interest of the Soviets. The reply I got was that the good folk of Samarqand should, as the Sart proverb has it, jolly well 'pour their water into their own buckets', and not meddle in the affairs of a friendly neighbouring state. I shrugged my shoulders and said that I personally had no concern with the domestic affairs of the individual Soviet states, but here I was in Tajikistan and I begged the comrades to take note of my presence.

I doubt if there was a single divisional president, high official, or commissar, or even an office boy, in Dushamba who did not think it his business to take cognisance of my unauthorised arrival. I should have been inclined to show a clean pair of heels and leave the worthy gentlemen to spend a year or so deciding under whose jurisdiction my singular case should be considered if the officials had not unfortunately impounded my papers. It would be useless to pretend that I looked on calmly at all this telegraphing to and fro. I did not. I was in a most almighty stew lest Samarqand had discovered my real identity and orders might be sent for my immediate arrest, or that some one had had the bright idea of making inquiries for Steinschneider in Qizil Arwat. Nothing of either sort in fact occurred. One fine day a militiaman turned up and requested me with the greatest politeness to come with him to the Soviet office. The chairman of the Council of the Tajikistan People's Commissars received me with a broad grin and assured me over and over again that he had let all those blokes in Samarqand understand once and for all that they had no right whatever to grant permission for stray people to travel in other people's territories. Thereupon he gave me a permit to reside and travel in the land of the Tajiks and the solemn assurance that my mineral specimens had been annexed by the Republic of Tajikistan and would certainly not be handed over to those of Uzbegistan.

I tried in vain to make it clear to the good man that by this procedure neither of the two countries would derive any benefit from my explorations, since my sketch maps and notes about the position of my discoveries were all on their way to Samarqand by post and that the notes without the specimens had no value whatever, since they were all numbered to correspond. Conversely the specimens had no value for Tajikistan without the notes explaining their exact provenance. To my amazement this information delighted the honourable gentleman so much that he burst into shouts of loud laughter, and then with inimitable gravity cried: 'Never mind; so much the better!'

Soviet red tape had held me up for a week, though a two days' ride would easily have taken me across the border into Uzbegistan. An excellent, newly made road leads from Dushamba to Hisar and on to Deh i Nau, crossing through the territory of the Masang

Dushamba. A dealer in birds of prey with hunting eagle

gipsies. What odd contrasts this world provides! With us the gipsies are a restless folk who trek hither and thither through Europe with their wheeled caravans. But here, in the land of nomads, the gipsies are settled people. As with us, however, they are looked down upon and considered an inferior race. So much so that, although the Masang women are famous for their beauty, no gipsy girl was in former times ever received into a harem. They have thus retained their racial purity without blood admixture of other stocks. They are artists and craftsmen, renowned as iron-founders, metal-workers, gold and silver-smiths. The Masang gipsies manufacture weapons, especially sabres, daggers, and battleaxes, which are famous throughout the whole country.

The valleys round Hisar have, however, yet another title to fame – they rejoice in more scorpions to the square foot than any other corner of Asia.

Nobody is likely to believe what multitudes of them there really are. When I spent the night in the *chai-khana* of Hisar hundreds of these revolting brutes were scrambling about the room so that it sounded as if a regiment of grasshoppers were dancing on a tight drum. Now was my chance to test the natives' assertion that scorpions never tread on felt. I slept on a felt blanket, and I can testify that I was not bitten nor even touched by one. As a general rule a scorpion will not attack a man unless it feels itself in danger. They love, however, to take refuge for the night in boots or in the sleeves of shirts. If you touch one when you are dressing, it naturally bites. The same thing may happen if you accidentally roll over on one in your sleep. Scientists call the scorpion of Turkistan *Androctonus asiaticus*, the 'Asiatic man-slayer', which sufficiently indicates its deadly efficiency.

Wherever scorpions thrive, tarantulas are also at home. The Turkistanis are more afraid of the tarantula than of the scorpion, believing that its bite is inevitably fatal. One day I was rigging up my primitive camp kitchen on the banks of the Dushamb and I lifted a few stones with which to build a fireplace. There was a whole nest of tarantulas under one of the stones, and after I had got over my initial terror I was able to observe them carefully. The tarantula's body is egg-shaped and from two to two and a quarter inches long. Its long, very hairy legs measure nearly four inches, and like its body vary from light yellow to brown. Its mouth is provided with sharp fangs and four jaws, which snap like lightning and inflict four simultaneous wounds, into which the poison is injected.

Driving along one day in my wheeled cart through southern Bukhara I fell in with a caravan, which passed through a large and gloriously fertile oasis without halting. I begged the caravan-*bashi* to pitch camp in the oasis. He assured me that if he did so not a man of us would be alive next morning, for we were within the area of the qarakurt spiders. I said I should very much like to see one, as I had heard so much about them. He dismounted cautiously and impaled on a camel thorn a small black something which he handed over to me. This was one of the dreaded qarakurt, not bigger than the nail of a man's finger, and yet capable of slaying any living man or beast within the space of a few minutes. The poison of this spider is absolutely deadly, and this is why many rich and luxuriant stretches of country in the valleys of the Ili and of the Amu Darya are uninhabited.

As I mentioned earlier I had got a severe dose of malaria into my system on the banks of the Amu Darya after crossing the Qara Qum. It remained in my blood and gave me a good deal of trouble from time to time on my way to the Alai. Once I reached higher altitudes these bouts of recurrent fever had ceased of themselves, but on the morning after my arrival in Hisar I was quivering so with ague that I could not get up. I found I still had some quinine in my little medicine chest. On the fourth day, in a lucid interval, I begged the owner of the serai to fetch me a doctor. But there was neither a Russian nor a Sart doctor to be found anywhere in Hisar or the neighbourhood. So there was nothing for it but to hie me back to Dushamba, where there was a hospital of sorts with a European doctor. They kindly bundled me on to a wheeled cart, tied me on with ropes, and sent me off. For four weeks I was consumed with raging fever. My body was nothing but a quinine magazine, but at last the quantities of quinine and of vodka that I had absorbed began to take effect. When I could think clearly again and even eat a little the doctor spent all his spare time at my bedside, and we often talked for hours together.

Thanks to his care and to the soundness of my constitution, the fever gradually yielded, and one day I actually got to the point of being able to leave my bed. When I got back to Hisar the owner of the serai did not recognise me, so completely had the malaria altered my appearance. I only finally shook it off in 1932, after its persistence had been the despair of several Vienna specialists. The forethought of the Dushamba physician provided me with half a pound of quinine for my further journey, and every morning, with heartfelt curses, I swallowed a dose of the bitterest of all powders. I owed it to this precaution, however, that during the rest of my travels I suffered only short and comparatively slight attacks.

From Hisar my course now led me to Qara Tagh, Sar i Asia, Yurtchi, and Deh i Nau, the scene of the last act of the Enver Pasha tragedy. Yurtchi was the birthplace of the last Qush Begi of Bukhara, and I hoped here to get some news of the man who had once so nobly befriended me. With great precaution I made inquiries about such well-to-do people as the village had known in earlier days, and when I had made their acquaintance I called on them in their homes. Gradually I ascertained that the Qush Begi had followed his master, the Amir of Bukhara, into exile in Afghanistan, and that he was believed to be still alive there. When the Bolsheviks broke up the Amir's harem after its master's hasty flight, the Qush Begi's daughter returned to her relatives in Deh i Nau. Unfortunately I was not able to trace her. Possibly the Bukharans were afraid lest if I claimed acquaintance it might in some way get her into trouble.

My efforts to find the sometime favourite of the Amir's harem, if it bore no other fruit, at least brought me into touch with a lot of people, and I found out that the Agabekoff of whom the Izfairan forester had told me was one of the biggest traders in the Deh i Nau bazaar. The rest was easy. I looked him up, as if by chance, and also by chance happened to speak of the fighting round Yurtchi and Deh i Nau. Swollen with pride over his own prowess and his heroic act of patriotism, Agabekoff told me everything I wanted to know about Enver Pasha's death. When I bade him farewell I happened – by chance of course – to overlook his outstretched hand without, I hoped, offending him. Some years later fate duly overtook him. For some political reason or other he had to fly the country, and he perished miserably in exile.

Two caravan roads lead out of Deh i Nau: one southwards by Sar Mak and Shirabad to Chuchka Guzar on the Amu Darya; the other westwards to Baisun, Tang i Khurram, and thence northwards via Guzar to Samarqand. I should have been glad to visit the Amir's old summer quarters in Shirabad, but I was more anxious to go to Guzar and on to Kelif. I felt I simply must see just once the town which years ago had been the longed-for goal that haunted night and day the dreams of an escaping prisoner of war. The roads ahead were in good condition, so I reluctantly decided to exchange my camel, at a well-known camel-breeder's, for a horse and wheeled cart. This transaction cost me the remainder of my ready cash.

The Turkistan arabah is a unique type of vehicle. It has two great wheels the height of a man, which never cease from squealing. Between them a massive frame is fixed, the front of which acts as the shafts for the horse. The axle, which is usually two or three yards long, is never directly fastened to the frame, but attached by strips of wood lashed with string, which act as rude springs. The horse is not only harnessed but saddled and the driver rides with his feet drawn up and resting on the shafts. The rims of the wooden wheels have no iron tyres and consequently soon wear out, but the size of the wheels is of great advantage in the sort of country over which they have to travel. Any other type of cart would certainly sink in and remain embedded to the axle in the deep mud of a Turkistan town. In fording rivers and streams – which, bridges being usually non-existent, is often the only means of crossing – the tall wheels are also invaluable.

From Deh i Nau onwards the road passes through deep gorges with lofty walls of rock on either side. I halted for my noonday rest at the Aq Su spring, where Enver had been murdered. A little wood lies just to the left of the caravan road in the middle of a small steppe-like valley. In front of it is the spring of water where the last act of the tragedy took place. Not a stone, not a memorial tablet marks the spot where one of the most remarkable generals of the World War met his death.

Baisun used to be a great Bukharan fortress guarding the valley of the Surkhan from the north-east. The place is surrounded by strong, high walls of mud, pierced by six great gates. Even to-day Baisun is the headquarters of an Uzbeg cavalry garrison a thousand strong. The Bolsheviks have great achievements to their credit in military matters, but, alas, they have not abolished the old martial music! Unfortunately for me the *chai-khana* where I spent the three nights of my stay lay just on the road by which the troops rode to their early morning exercises, so that I got the thumping and caterwauling at first hand. In the van rode thirty men armed with kettledrums, followed by an equal number of players on the pipe, and these again by twenty lusty fellows with drums. These eighty 'musicians' beat or blew their instruments just as their individual fancy took them. The squeaking and squawking of the pipes, the sharp 'rattatatting' of the kettledrums, and the deeper thudding of the drums produced a chaos of discordant sound that almost amounted to genius. I never reckoned myself a connoisseur of the arts, and this music wrought me nearly to frenzy.

While in Baisun I accidentally heard from a Russian who had been living in the place since 1920 the history of the *chai-khana-chik* in whose house I was lodging: he was no less a man than the once omnipotent Beg of the whole Darband district, whose official headquarters had been here in Baisun. He was one of the few of the more important Bukharan officials who had not taken flight when the country was bolshevized. He had had the wit to adapt himself to altered circumstances and since – in contrast to most of his colleagues – he enjoyed a measure of popularity amongst the people, he had been left unmolested. With his own hands he had built himself a very handsome little *chai-khana*, which he kept most scrupulously clean. Again with his own hands he brewed tea for his customers, grilled *shishlik*, and prepared *pulau* to the general satisfaction. When one thinks that a few years before this man had had a staff of a hundred servants at his disposal and that his former palace still stood in full view of his modest inn and was now the seat of the local Soviet offices, one cannot help admiring both the physical achievement and the moral courage of the fellow.

I now devoted somewhat more attention to the erstwhile Beg. When he discovered that I was neither a Russian nor a Bolshevik I soon succeeded in gaining his confidence, and I owe to him a lot of extremely interesting information about the ancient political structure of the Amirate of Bukhara, most of which is known only to the initiate.

Each beg was the highest executive and judicial authority in the district assigned to him by the Amir. He had full, independent power to appoint his officials and judges – naturally relations or favourites of his own. On the death or recall of a beg every courtier and official automatically lost his job, since the new beg was in honour bound to give his own friends and relatives the benefit of whatever offices and dignities were going. The Amir arbitrarily laid down the taxes and payments to be made to him, and it was the beg's business to raise these and pay then in person to the Amir.

To meet these demands the beg had naturally to squeeze the people, and since he received no pay from the Amir and was responsible for the maintenance of the military, the police, the irrigation overseers and all necessary road repairs, he naturally had to squeeze them further to cover his expenses, besides providing a decent income for himself and his court. Knowing that his term of office depended solely on the caprice of the Amir, each beg devoted all his energies to making hay for himself while the sun shone – at the expense of course of his unhappy subjects.

145

The oases of Bukhara often lie hundreds of miles apart, so that the various begs enjoyed great independence. So much indeed that they not infrequently waged war against each other in order to increase the area subject to their oppression.

The beg's court was modelled in every detail on the royal Court in Bukhara. Each beg had his own prime minister or *diwan begi*; next in importance ranked the cupbearer and tax collector, then the master of the horse; after him came the commander of the bodyguard, and finally the *mirza-bashi* or private secretary. Each of these major officials maintained, of course, a squad of servants for his own comfort and convenience, while the beg himself had a host of minor retainers: clerks, cooks, grooms, astrologers, policemen, bootboys, drivers, men to saddle his horses, men to carry his tablecloths, eunuchs, jugglers, magicians, dancers, musicians, and others too numerous to mention. A small province of perhaps only twenty, thirty, or forty thousand inhabitants had to bear the burden of supporting this inflated court and administration. It is not hard to see why the seed of Communism fell on fertile soil amongst the poor of Bukhara.

In Bukhara the hallmark of good breeding is leisurely, dignified movement, which must be maintained even when travelling. The average day's journey considered suitable for a Bukharan dignitary used to be a stage of barely over five miles. These stages were called 'tash' (stone or hill), because the soldiers sent in advance of their master used to erect every five miles or so a small dais of stones about three feet high, on which the beg's tent would be pitched for the night. So it comes about that the five-mile tash is the unit of distance in Bukhara for measuring roads or estimating journeys. Even in the face of danger it would be impossible for a Bukharan aristocrat to contemplate travelling at greater speed.

I was also greatly interested in the method in which the begs paid over their annual tribute to the Amir. My informant, the last Beg of Baisun, had paid over his last tribute on the 16th of April 1920. It consisted of:

146

70 horses with silver-plated harness and stirrups set with turquoise;

100 robes of honour: 20 each of satin, silk, gold brocade,
cashmere, and cotton;

500 pieces of silk material;

5,000 tanga of gold and silver (a tanga equals about 10 kopeks),
say 500 roubles;

25 silver girdles set with turquoise;

100 batman each of rice, millet, wheat, and barley, say 288 lb.
each, avoirdupois;

50 transport camels

2 dasir of unminted gold, say 145 lb. avoirdupois;

5 dasir of unminted silver, say 362 lb. avoirdupois.

The Baisun province has a population of approximately 90,000
souls who had to cough up, not only the expenses of their begs,
but in addition this stately tribute to the Amir. My beg assured me
that this tribute was by no means the heaviest in the country.

The begs naturally dreaded like the very devil these tribute
journeys of theirs. Not one of them knew whether he would be
allowed to return to his post or not. His very existence hung on
the favour of the Amir, the intrigues of his favourites, and the
accident of whether the ruler chose to be pleased or not with the
quality of the tribute offered. Many a beg set out for Bukhara in
the full sunshine of royal favour – and never returned. Either the
executioner had received the order 'Off with his head!' or the
luckless fellow was slowly rotting in one of the Amir's dungeons,
which were never known to relinquish their prey. To try and keep
in the Amir's good graces a beg was forced to curry favour with
the higher Court officials and the favourites of the day by making
princely gifts to them, for a single word from one of them was often
sufficient to cause his downfall. The beg's subjects had of course to
be further bled in order to supply the necessary bribes.

When the Amir Saiyid Muzaffar ud Din died in 1886 his
successor Saiyid Ahad Khan summoned all the begs to Bukhara.

Thirty-two of them responded to the command. Eighteen were executed and thirteen imprisoned, so that the new Amir could replace them by his own nominees. Only one was reinstated in his office. All the property of the ex-begs was, incidentally, confiscated.

When I again took the road I travelled through the lovely mountain country of the Hisar range to Qara Khoval and Tang i Khurram and southwards over the last outliers of the mountains down into the fruitful valley of the Amu Darya to Kelif on the Afghan border. In 1916 I had escaped from the prison camp of Katta Qurghan, but had the bad luck to lose my way south of Guzar, so that instead of making Kelif, as I had intended, I ran straight into the arms of the Bukharan police, who surrendered me to the Russians. I now turned my cart into the caravan road which was then to have led me to freedom. Beside the spring of Kuh i Tang I bivouacked again in the open – for the first time for months. There were some Sarts living in mud huts in the neighbourhood, but the look of their miserable little hovels made me shudder. Late the following night my cart rumbled and clattered over a bridge and across a stream, and half an hour later I was halting at the door of a serai in Kelif.

On the road I had overtaken a lot of carts laden with red rock-salt, bringing the natural wealth of the mountains down to the valley. The southern slopes of the mountains facing the Amu are rich in various kinds of ore. Gold, iron, copper, lead, sulphur, and turquoise have been dug out here for centuries, without there having been any systematic attempt at mining. Whatever cannot easily be lifted from day to day is left to lie, and is thus preserved for future generations.

Above Kelif the Amu Darya is broken by great, impassable rapids, so that steamers make Kelif their last port of call. The last steamer of the year happened to come up while I was staying there. After August river navigation is possible only as far as Kerki, for however shallow their draught, ships are liable to strand on shoals and sandbanks. Despite its great width, the Amu is a shallow river. During the summer season when the melting of the snows is at its maximum, the river brings down from Sari Kul (Lake Victoria), lying high up on the Pamirs at 13,000 feet, hundreds of thousands of cubic yards of sand and mud, with which it clutters up its bed. The banks are thinly populated and the steamer service is a poorly paying business which has only been started in fairly recent times.

The ships plying on the Amu Darya at that time had previously seen service on the Sir Darya, a river where mud-silting is even speedier and more serious. The ships were originally built in Germany to order of the tsarist government, but the specifications sent were incorrect. They drew too much water. Without their being remeasured they were sent down the Sir Darya to the Sea of Aral and up the Amu, and are expected to do the best they can to find a navigable channel for themselves. It often happens that a boat will take a fortnight or more to do the stretch between Kerki and Charjui, which is the most mud-ridden of all. The most moderate horseman can cover the distance in well under one day, so you will not be surprised to learn that the steamers are not much used for passenger traffic. I did this journey myself by boat in 1916 as a prisoner. Our ship, the *Tsar Alexander*, took six days, which the captain considered an unusually favourable record.

On the present occasion I hastened to apply direct to the captain of the *Red Turkmenistan*, and ascertained that his ship was leaving in three days for Petro Alexandrovsk. I asked whether he would be prepared to give a free passage to a State geologist. He retorted by asking if I played chess. I gladly said 'Yes'. Thereupon he explained that in that case he would be delighted to take me on any terms, even free of charge. Emboldened by this success I suggested that perhaps he would also be kind enough to carry my horse and cart for nothing, to which he also agreed.

So I took my place on the deck of the white-painted, dazzlingly clean little ship, let my feet dangle over the side towards the Afghan shore, and looked across at the farther bank which had once been the goal of so much passionate desire. How different my life would have been had I struck the river here that time instead of seventy-five miles farther west! The captain came and sat beside me, offered

149

me cigarettes, and began to talk. He had been plying for thirty-two years up and down the thousand miles or so of navigable river between Kelif and the Sea of Aral, and had served on each of the four steamers that did the run. He had been captain of the *Tsar Alexander* from 1911 to 1920 – this made me prick up my ears – which the Bukharans set fire to when she was at anchor in Ulam. Her charred hull was still lying alongside the bank. When we passed her a few days later I gazed on the wreck with something akin to homesickness. It was the very ship which had carried me back, after my abortive dash for freedom, to the dungeons of Charjui.

In Kerki I bade good-bye to my eccentric friend, the river captain, carrying off an ample supply of cigarettes which I had won from him at chess. My cart and nag were dragged ashore with much difficulty. In 1916 you had had to wade through the marsh to the ship, but now a wooden pier jutted far out into the river, and I could disembark dryshod. There was a *chai-khana* near the landing stage, and I confided my horse to the care of its owner, while I myself climbed the loess hill which led to the former castle of the Beg, later the seat of the Qush Begi.

Great red flags were fluttering in the wind from both towers of the entrance gate. The Amir's arms had been torn down and replaced by the hammer and sickle; only the bare mud walls and a pair of prehistoric muzzle-loading guns stood unchanged since my previous visit. The former fortress now housed the local Soviet of Kerki under the chairmanship of Madame Kuliyeva. How the world changes! Madame Kuliyeva had been up till 1920 the veiled slave-woman of one Ali Yusuf, a rice merchant. After the Revolution she had been one of the first women to offer her services to the Soviet, and had shown so much initiative and organising ability that she had been appointed chairman of the local Soviet – a position equivalent to mayor or burgomaster. I paid a call on the lady, a woman of about forty, and found her a most able and energetic person, not in the least embarrassed in admitting that she had first learnt to read and write three years ago. She knew no other language than Uzbeg, but she was spending three hours a day

150

Madame Kuliyeva, chairman of the local Soviet of Kerki

working hard at Russian so as to be able to converse with Russians. She gave me an order for food on the Soviet co-operative store, which I did not scruple to make use of, the more gratefully that Ramazan began the day after my arrival and without the order I might easily have starved.

Ramazan is the Muslims' month-long fast and it is a nightmare to all the non-Muhammadan inhabitants of Turkistan. Possibly it had its origin in religious and hygienic ideas, but with the centuries it has become an ineradicable feature of Islamic observance. Communist teaching has been powerless to abolish it. The authorities even close the Government offices during the fast, and only the military can afford to ignore it. In earlier days all fighting ceased during Ramazan, and as late as the summer of 1918 the Amir sent an envoy to the Russians to request them to agree to a truce during the fast, as his soldiers could only fight at night.

During the month of the fast the true Muslim must neither eat nor drink from sunrise to sunset. He must not even wash nor take physic, he may not even smell a flower or smoke a cigarette, for nothing whatever is permitted to enter the body. The Muslim Fast bears no resemblance to our European fasts. It does not consist in merely refraining from meat food or in any such trifling modifications of diet, it imposes complete and unqualified abstinence during the hours of daylight. In the burning heat of Turkistan the ban on water is particularly severe. No sooner has the sun set, however, than eating and drinking begin with a vengeance and the quantities of food consumed seem almost incredible. Singing, dancing, and music continue all night through, and fireworks are let off. Towards dawn, when the Ramazan drum sounds through the streets, the orgy reaches its height, for every one hastily stuffs himself with as much as he can possibly hold, the better to endure through the coming day. Naturally the provision shops and eating-places in the bazaar are all closed by day. No Uzbeg nor Sart would cook or even handle food while daylight lasts.

As the co-operative supplied the small garrison of Kerki with food I was able to view the inconveniences of Ramazan with detachment as long as I stayed in the town. But I could hardly put in a whole month there. So one night, armed with a little ready money which Chairman Kuliyeva had given me from State resources, I made my purchases in the bazaar, fetched my horse out of its stable, and set out on the road to Qarshi. I very soon regretted having brought the cart. The wheels sank deep into the desert sand and most of the wells were dry. It is true that I had brought two sheepskins of water, which I refilled whenever opportunity offered, but the salty water of the desert wells served only to accentuate my thirst instead of relieving it. The shortage of water became so acute that I finally abandoned my cart in the middle of the desert, to save at least myself and my horse by flight.

Qarshi used in olden days to be one of the summer resorts

of the Amir. On arrival there I went down with another severe
attack of fever. There was a Russian colony of about twenty
people in Qarshi, boasting a Russian assistant doctor among them.
He succeeded in curing me at least sufficiently to enable me to
face the desert ride from Qarshi to Qara Kul – another 'Black Lake',
not of course to be confused with the Great Qara Kul on the

Kerki. A night dance during Ramazan

Pamirs, where I had spent the winter with my Qirghiz hosts. In
the course of our conversation I learnt that the doctor had been
taken prisoner by the Austrians during the war and had been
interned at Knittelfeld in Styria, where he had learnt to talk a little
German.

Qarshi is a typical desert town situated at the confluence of
several of those little salt streams which unexpectedly spring out of
the desert, flow along awhile, and then vanish into the sands again,
ending as mysteriously as they begin. They flow in a star-shaped
pattern round the town. The oasis is therefore not afflicted with

the shortage of water that is so frequent in other places in Bukhara. The whole neighbourhood is intersected by irrigation channels bringing ample water everywhere. The fertility and productivity of Qarshi and the quality of its fruits are famous throughout Uzbegistan. Rice, corn, lucerne, cotton, grapes, figs, apricots, pomegranates, and peaches weighing a pound apiece, often rot in the fields and on the trees for lack of sufficient buyers to benefit by the over-luxuriant harvest. Mountains of sweet melons and water-melons, as well as raisins, are piled in the bazaar and can be purchased for a song.

I sold my horse to the *chai-khana-chik* with whom I was putting up, so as to raise enough money to pay for the caravan journey to Qara Kul. I might have had to put in three weeks in Qarshi if I had had to wait till Ramazan was over and some goods caravan would be starting. By great good luck, however, a military column of mounted camelry were setting out in the Karnap Chöl direction to relieve the Desert Police. At my request the commandant agreed to take me with them as far as Chandir, which lies on the railway between Charjui and Bukhara. This arrangement would save me many inconveniences, not least the long delay.

Strangely enough, the commandant was a Russian – an ex-tsarist officer no less – who had served in Qaghan during the War. On the march I chatted with him about politics and economics. His Uzbeg men knew no Russian, so he felt it safe to discuss even the most dangerous topics with considerable freedom. His was the typical story of the Russian intelligence officer overtaken by the Revolution. Whether he felt in sympathy with Communist ideals or not, the instinct for self-preservation prompted him to offer allegiance to the new regime. He had tried to earn a living as interpreter, shoemaker and even coolie, but had finally reverted to his original profession of soldier. He was in possession of authentic facts and could take a detached view of the activities of the new rulers. I learnt many interesting things from him.

Turkistan has no industries and consequently no proletariat, and

Bolshevism caused therefore an even greater upheaval than in Russia.

The Bolsheviks were forced artificially to create the prerequisites for their propaganda. They first flooded the country with regulations, proclamations, and rallying cries. They formed a staff of professional agitators. Next, factories, co-operatives, peasant organisations, and workshops had to be created in the deserts and oases of Turkistan so as to conjure up class-consciousness where none had been before. The most grotesque attempts were made in fact to call the non-existent proletariat into being.

Up till 1920 Bukhara had been the most peaceful country in the world; shut in by its illimitable deserts of sand it had preserved its age-old traditions unaltered. Untainted by contact with European civilisation, it was the empire of a despotic Amir, who ruled in his citadel of Bukhara undisturbed by rebellions or governmental crises.

Sole and unquestioned autocrat of this great land, the Amir lived in his fortress on its dominating hill and ruled after the time-honoured custom of his predecessors. All day long officials, courtiers, officers, and dignitaries mixed with the people in the magic circle round the palace, awaiting the commands of their master. No man dared to pass the entrance gate without thrice prostrating himself to the ground.

Suddenly, in a night, all was changed. The people of Bukhara were roused from sleep by the thunder of their own and the Russian guns, and when they ventured out of their mud houses they learned that their Amir was no more and that another force had seized the reins – the Young Bukharans. The allies who had lent a hand against the despot soon showed their hand. The Young Bukharans, enemies of tradition, friends of progress and of Western culture, had only been temporary tools. They were soon brushed aside to make way for Russians, selected, hard-boiled Communists, who were installed in all offices and positions of authority. Madrasahs and mosques were taken out of their hands and converted into assembly halls and centres of agitation, in which skilled orators preached the glories of Communism. New and mysterious words: organisation, manufacture, redistribution of land, equality of rights, flew from mouth to mouth like magic spells, at the sound of which men shook and trembled. Great caravans, piled high with sheets of propaganda and revolutionary slogans, travelled in the charge of agitators from oasis to oasis and spread the new gospel – or at least strove to spread it. Laws were promulgated forbidding the veiling of women. The black cap, the widow's badge of shame, was abolished by decree, and agricultural machines which the Communists had for years been promising to the peasants of Russia, were packed off first into Central Asia to create an impression.

The whole Moscow programme, drawn up on so grandiose a scale and at such great expense, was wrecked on the *chimat*, the women's horse-hair veil. The menfolk of Bukhara were ready to adapt themselves to any changes: but the unveiling of their women was unthinkable. This law knocked the bottom out of the Soviet boat. Bukhara refused to be intimidated by the soldiers of the Red Army, by their machine-guns, by their quick-firing artillery. Rebellion flamed forth, from north to south, from east to west. Oasis after oasis arrested the Russian Commissars and the battle-cry: 'Bukhara for the Uzbegs!' spread through the mud towns with the speed of a prairie fire. Enver Pasha, supported by the powerful secret society of the Ishana, seized his opportunity and fanned the flames with great astuteness. He did not live to reap the harvest he had sown, but a mighty wave of rebellion swept Turkistan from end to end, and Moscow was compelled, with good grace or bad, to make concessions; for a Central Asia in perpetual revolt and kept in hand only by force would have shattered the whole constructive programme of the Union of Socialist Soviet Republics. And so, during the very months that I had been touring Persia and purchasing carpets for Qannadi, the various 'independent' republics of Uzbegistan, Tajikistan, Turkmenistan, and Qirghizistan had come to birth, while the former Khanate of Khiwa was once more endowed with its historic title of Khwarizm (the Chorasmia of Herodotus). With gnashing of teeth Moscow proclaimed these states autonomous and for the future treated them to some extent as such. Their independence is of course controlled and politically influenced from Moscow.

The first legislative act of the new Asian republics was to revoke the law relating to women's veils, and to restore many original place-names which the Russians in the first intoxication of imagined victory had called after famous characters of the Revolution. Many of these stank in the nostrils of Turkistan, and were duly blotted off the map. Freedom of religion was restored, and the law of Islam was in part incorporated in the law of the land.

These, and many other things, my Russian informant told me as we rode from Qarshi to Kasan, Mashhad, and Khadi Mubor towards Chandir. The old, well-trodden caravan road seemed dead. We met only a few caravans bringing ironware and petroleum from Bukhara to the south. The desert we were riding through is in no way different from the great desert of the Qara Qum – sand and nothing but sand as far as eye can see. When the low mud towers of a well are sighted, man and beast rejoice at the thought of water, though the wells in this region contain more salt than anywhere else in Asia. But the water is at least cool and a draught of it gives the momentary illusion of quenching thirst. No sooner have you mounted again, however, and begun to sweat than thirst returns worse than before. At such moments a drink of sweet water or a piece of clean ice seems the highest attainable earthly bliss.

It is amazing on how little the people of the desert contrive to live. There is here not a sign of the rich flocks and herds you see in the oases; a few bony, half-starved sheep and an occasional skinny cow are the only cattle owned by some hundreds of people – apart, of course, from the indispensable camels. There is no fruit; there are no melons. Millet and barley are the only crops and yet these folk love their bit of ground and would not leave it.

After Khadi Mubor the road runs through a completely waterless stretch of eighty-five miles or so, and water must be carried. Fortunately the wells of Khadi Mubor are less salty than the others, but the water from them must be purchased. The water-tax of

twenty kopeks (about 4½d.) per waterskin is the only source of
revenue the oasis possesses. The assistant doctor who was attached
to our column had a thermometer with him which he set in the
shade of a wall. It registered 125.6 degrees F. in the shade. The hot
air flickered in the intolerable heat and there was not a breath of
wind stirring. The inhabitants of Mashhad bemoaned the fact that
the heat had been so great that their stocks of dung-fuel had
spontaneously caught fire and they would now be left fireless all
the winter and would freeze to death. Our commandant promised
to report the case to the Soviet in Bukhara and have some fuel sent
to them before the winter if he could.

To evade this terrific heat the commandant decided that we
should only march at night. We started off as darkness fell, the
thermometer then reading 95 degrees F. The worst day of all was
our halt on the 4th of August. The soldiers had fixed their bayonets
and plunged them in the ground, spreading the tent canvas over
the stocks of their inverted rifles in order to get a little shade. If by
chance you touched any metal object you dropped it at once with
a cry – it blistered the hand. The rifles had to be unloaded. Cartridge
belts and the ammunition for our three machine-guns were buried
in the sand at some distance from the camp for fear of their
exploding of themselves. We also buried our waterskins, lest they
should burst and waste our priceless water. Weary and worn out as
we were, none of us could sleep. Soldiers and animals alike rolled
restlessly about, groaning. If robbers or rebels had surprised us, not
a soul would have had strength to offer resistance. At last the
merciless sun went down and within a quarter of an hour the night
was pitch dark. Cursing and swearing the men loaded up their
animals, a ration of water was issued for each, and the camels were
urged to speed so that we might reach the gold-laden Zarafshan by
dawn.

It was an interminable night. I refrained from asking the doctor
fellow what his thermometer said. What was the use? With or
without a thermometer the heat was equally intolerable. No one
spoke a word the whole night through. I doubt if anyone was

capable of formulating a coherent thought, so dog-tired were we all.

It was getting towards morning when, without any encouragement from their riders, the camels suddenly quickened their pace and presently broke into a crazy gallop. Half an hour's march – five miles away – they had scented the river and there was no holding them. Joyously we gave them their head, not sorry ourselves to have escaped from hell. In vain the commandant warned us about snakes. Each man tore off his clothes, leapt into the shallow river, and drank till he could drink no more. Then we merrily splashed each other like little children and shouted for sheer joy.

In Chandir I bade a warm farewell to the commandant, who, poor chap, had to lead his men out again into the red-hot desert, while I was heading for the gardens and pools of Bukhara. Again and again he said what a pleasure it had been to meet another European. It would certainly be many months before he could get away to Samarqand or Bukhara and mix with his own kind again. As a parting gift he presented me with a box of cigarettes.

Chandir possesses no railway station. It used to be an optional halt and trains could be stopped on request, but now that there was only one train a day it had been cut out. I had spotted an old trolley lying in a ruined railway shed. I opened my box of cigarettes in the hope of bribing the railway man into compliance with my plans. Imagine my amazement to find a twenty-rouble note on top! It wasn't likely that the Russian cigarette makers had taken to packing twenty-rouble notes into each box of cigarettes; I could only conclude that the money was a gift from the thoughtful donor, who had thus chosen unobtrusively to help my finances. With this and the hundred and ten roubles I had got for my horse in Qarshi, I was now free of money anxieties for some time to come. I spent ten roubles on acquiring the right to ride on the trolley as far as Qara Kul, where there was a station at which the trains stopped.

As soon as it was dark, I placed my scanty kit on the trolley, seized the lever, and began to work it to and fro with all my might.

Whatever sins I have committed I must have expiated the bulk of them that night. I was out of training and I groaned and coughed under the exertion necessary to keep the wretched trolley moving. I often stopped and ran down to the Zarafshan to have a drink and souse my body with the cool water. At long last I spied the dark outline of an unlit railway station in front of me. I had arrived in Qara Kul, the oasis which has given its name to the valuable lambskins.

Almost all travellers in Turkistan have let themselves be tempted into retailing terrible horrors connected with the process of procuring these skins. Even the Viennese Jacques Jäger, whose book appeared in 1903, writes: 'The method of extracting the unborn-lamb skins from the mother sheep is so cruel that I dare not harrow the reader's feelings by describing it.'

Similar statements are frequent. It is noteworthy, however, that no two of these eye and ear witnesses – for such they pretend to be – describe these alleged cruelties in the same way. Each appears to have witnessed a different method, or else they are silent about details and record only that terrible cruelty is practised.

I have been three times in Bukhara myself and I have lived for seven years in Turkistan, amongst other places in the Katta Qurghan district, which, next to Qara Kul itself, is the most important breeding centre for Qara Kul sheep, and never once have I seen any process entailing the slightest cruelty to animals. The pelt of the Qara Kul sheep – wrongly called Persian, or Astrakhan, or Fat-Tail in Europe – appears to reach its best condition in the two oases of Qara Kul and Katta Qurghan. All attempts to breed these sheep successfully in Persia or China have conspicuously failed, though the breeders even tried to transplant the animals' favourite food, a kind of wild corn. The breeders of Qara Kul attribute the delicate, tight curls of the pelt, which give it its peculiar value, to the fact that their sheep eat this wild corn, which grows only in these two places in Turkistan and refuses to thrive elsewhere. As soon as the sheep are transferred to another place the pelts lose all their characteristic qualities. The lambskins are mostly exported via

Persia or Astrakhan, a fact which no doubt accounts for the inaccurate names given them in Europe.

While I was staying in Qara Kul I took time and trouble to investigate this question and see for myself the method by which the skins are procured. Contrary to the prevailing rumour, the pregnant ewes are treated with the greatest care and tenderness, especially in the last days before the lambs are born. The mother sheep are far too valuable to be sacrificed or maltreated in any way. And the infant lambs are likewise handled with affectionate attention. They are killed on the fourth to eighth day. The little pelt is at once wrapped in salt and barley flour to preserve the curls. It is therefore an absolute myth that the ewe's belly is cut open while she is still alive and that the lamb must be slaughtered while still warm in its mother's womb in order to preserve the beauty of the skin.

XII

Bukhara the Noble

F rom Qara Kul I proceeded some fifty miles by rail to Bukhara. The railway runs in an absolutely straight line through richly cultivated country to the small *qishlaq* of Qaghan, which is the junction for the branch line to Bukhara. The last time I had stayed in Qaghan it was a modest little spot which, apart from the barracks which belonged to the Russian Frontier Force, boasted only two European buildings, the residence of the District Commandant and the main livery stables, which were in private hands. The concessionaire in those days was a German named Schmid, whose neighbour, the apothecary Reinhard – also a German – proved a great benefactor to the prisoners of war in Katta Qurghan and Samarqand.

Just as in my old prisoner-of-war days, there were carriages standing in front of the railway station, waiting to be hired. But reasons of economy led me to prefer travelling to Bukhara by rail. In olden days the railway was never used and it had been destroyed by the Bukharans, but since 1922 it has again been in action. Two trains a day ran to the station in front of the main city gate of Bukhara. The little train consisted of one engine and two coaches and it proceeded at a very leisurely and comfortable pace, finally coming to a halt just under the city wall.

Bukhara was once the largest and most powerful empire in Trans-Oxiana and centralised all its wealth and glory in its capital city, which was known until 1920 as 'Bukhara the Holy'. The Russians were reluctant to rob it completely of an impressive epithet and it is now entitled 'Bukhara the Noble'.

162

The city is extremely ancient. A considerable settlement is known to have existed here more than three thousand years ago. In the course of her history Bukhara has been repeatedly destroyed and rebuilt. Under the rule of the Arabs she attained to immense wealth.

Two hundred and fifteen years after the Hijra (A.D. 622) Abd ul Abbas built the city wall, which is standing to this day. He raised it as a protection against the ever-present threat of Turkoman

Bukhara. Left: the Mir Arab Madrasah; right: the Kalan Masjid; between them the Tower of Death

attacks, for the wealth of the city acted as a constant lure to raiders. Then the Arabs became masters, and they laid out the greater part of the huge system of artificial irrigation channels between the Amu Darya and the Zarafshan which still serve the city and its environs.

Some conception of the immense wealth of the city can be formed from the ancient writings, which tell that it paid an annual tribute of 200,000 dirhems to the Khalif of Baghdad. Under the Samanids Bukhara paid taxes to the tune of over a million dirhems.

PLAN OF BUKHARA

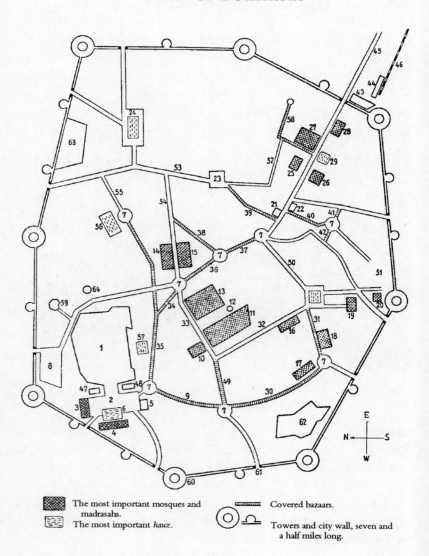

The most important mosques and madrasahs.

The most important *hauz*.

Covered bazaars.

Towers and city wall, seven and a half miles long.

PLAN OF BUKHARA

1. Ark, Citadel.
2. Rigistan.
3. Madrasah Gusfand.
4. Madrasah Shadibik.
5. Barracks.
6. *Hauz* of Rigistan.
7. Char Su bazaars.
8. Standing place for carts, and fodder bazaar.
9. Silk and shoe bazaar.
10. Mosque of Harun ar Rashid.
11. Kalan Mosque.
12. Tower of Death.
13. Madrasah Mir Arab.
14. Madrasah Ulugh Beg.
15. Madrasah Abd ul Aziz.
16. Madrasah.
17. Mosque Ismail Khoja.
18. Mosque.
19. Mosque Mir Khoja.
20. Mosque.
21. Serai.
22. Furs, charcoal, and *khilat* bazaar.
23. Books and paper bazaar.
24. *Hauz* and baths.
25. Mosque Khalif Niaz.
26. Mosque Diwan Begi.
27. Madrasah and Mosque Gök Tash.
28. Madrasah Diwan Begi.
29. *Hauz* Diwan Begi.
30. Ironware bazaar.
31. Cotton and rice bazaar.
32. Embroidery, silk, carpets, and cloth bazaar.
33. Qarakul bazaar.
34. Carpet and shoe bazaar.
35. Coppersmiths' and bakers' bazaar.
36. *Khilat* and corn bazaar.
37. Money-changers' and cutlers' bazaar.
38. Goldsmiths' and jewellers' bazaar.
39. Turban bazaar and teahouses.
40. Butchers', saddlers', and china bazaar.
41. Weapon-smiths' and wheelwrights' bazaar.
42. Doctors' and apothecaries' bazaar.
43. Amir's New Castle.
44. Railway station.
45. Road to Qaghan and frontier.
46. Railway to Qaghan.
47. Barracks of Bodyguard.
48. Artillery Arsenal.
49. Wood and straw bazaar.
50. Sweetmeat, egg, and fowl bazaar.
51. Cemetery.
52. Salt and provisions bazaar.
53. Carpenters' bazaar.
54. Street of dyers and weavers.
55. Street of rope and cord makers.
56. *Hauz.*
57. *Hauz.*
58. Potters' bazaar.
59. New Prison.
60. Fortress tower.
61. City gate.
62. Jews' Quarter.
63. Leper Quarter.
64. Zindan, Old Prison.

Bukhara was also the centre of Islamic culture and oriental handicrafts. The silks and clothing materials which were there produced were accounted the most valuable and the most beautiful in all Asia, and their fame extended to Arabia, Persia, and Egypt, and even as far as Greece. In those days only three dyes were known in Bukhara, white, red, and green. Only vegetable dyes were employed, for animal and, of course, artificial chemical dyes were unknown. Next to her costly materials, her carpets carried the fame of Bukhara far and wide through the Islamic world. The Bukharan carpets of those days were so valuable that the town could remit its tribute of 200,000 dirhems to Baghdad in the form of one single carpet.

Under the successors of the Arabs Bukhara fell on evil days, until Timur the Lame brought a new era of glory. At his court in Samarqand he assembled artists from every quarter of the known world, and with their assistance he erected buildings the like of which had never before been dreamed of. The last of the great Timurids, the royal astronomer Ulugh Beg, also devoted himself to Bukhara and built a large number of magnificent mosques and madrasahs.

It was assuredly neither mere vanity nor self-conceit which prompted the people of Bukhara to ask the traveller Vambéry: 'Haji, you have seen many lands. Now tell us, is there in all the world any city so beautiful as Bukhara?' The unspoiled beauty of the city had indeed no rival.

Until the Bolshevik conquest, Bukhara was the only isolated oasis which was the home of oriental culture and the spirit of Islam. The ancient city walls with their watchtowers and loopholes would have been small protection against the tide of Western influence; a more potent guardian of Bukhara's integrity was the historic rivalry of England and Russia, both of whom cast jealous eyes on the hub of Central Asia. The Amirs of Bukhara were masters in the art of playing the one off against the other for their own advantage, so that Bukhara's independence and individuality were thus more effectively protected than the Middle Empire of China by its Great Wall.

The available space inside the town is restricted, and every inch of it is turned to good account. This has kept foreign intruders at bay. Even the excess native population is forced to quit the town and seek new means of livelihood in the outskirts. Probably no oriental city has ever been so completely in the hands of religious fanatics as Bukhara. The power of mullas and muftis was unlimited. As late as 1919, when I was in the city, officers of the faith used regularly to patrol the streets and bazaars, hold up the passers-by, and cross-question them about any chance *surah* of the Quran or the laws of the Shariah. If the luckless Believer could give no satisfactory answer the officer would order his police escort to arrest and carry him off, issuing a warning to any others who might prove inadequately versed in their sacred book. Punishment took the form either of a beating or a fine.

The city had eleven gates, which were closed at nightfall, and any movement to and fro within the city after this hour was forbidden under heavy penalty. From the outbreak of the World War till 1920 the city gates were closed all day as well, and no one could pass through without producing a special permit. Nowadays the gates are open day and night and there are no restrictions whatever on people's movements.

The life of the night-watchman in Bukhara has, however, undergone no change. Hundreds of them still wander through the streets, as they have always done, protecting the quarter of the city allotted to their care. Each watchman is equipped with a cudgel, which he bangs several times on the gate of every courtyard as he passes by – thus intimidating would-be law-breakers of every kind. The noise of the watchmen's knocking echoes through the streets, and serves the double purpose of reassuring the householders – proving that the watchmen are really awake and that they are earning their pay – and scaring off burglars. I suppose the system works, since it continues. The watchman is, however, bound by the strict general law forbidding any one to enter another person's house.

The system of night-watching in the bazaars is even more peculiar. All the streets in the bazaars are roofed in as a protection against the sun, and every couple of hundred yards they are provided with skylights. Through these you can look down on the booth-like shops below. The night-watchman walks along the tops of the roofs like an invisible guardian angel, beating his drum without intermission and peering down at intervals through the holes to observe the effect of his procedure.

None of the watchmen carry arms and those posted on the roofs could only get down into the streets by long roundabout ways if they did want to arrest a thief, so the effect of their activities must be moral rather than practical. The desired result, however, is achieved and the fact remains that theft and burglary are the rarest of all crimes in Bukhara.

Next to Samarqand, Bukhara was and still is the largest commercial centre of Central Asia. A great part of the city is taken up by serais and caravanserais. These used formerly to be either the property of the Amir or else pious foundations; they are now under the direction of the Uzbeg Soviet. These serais may perhaps best be compared to our customs houses and warehouses. They are usually one or two stories high and are built round a large central court. The court and the lower rooms serve as storerooms, the upper ones as offices and shops. An open terrace, like a verandah corridor, runs right round the front of the upper story and all the doors open on to it. Summer and winter alike the individual doors all stand open, for windows are unknown and the door is the only source of light.

Most of Bukhara's bazaars date from her earlier days of glory – the Char Su for instance, under one of the great cupolas, and the somewhat similar Goldsmiths' Bazaar which was built by Abd ul Aziz Khan of the Shaiban dynasty. Linked to these are the bazaars for books, padded quilts, shoes, ironware, ornaments, leather, stuffs, felt rugs, silks, and velvets, carpets, pottery, furs, and turbans. In between are ranged the booths of the butchers, dyers, money-changers, tinsmiths, tanners, and smiths; then follow the salt and charcoal dealers, the bakers and fruit-sellers, the waggoners and wheelwrights, whose booths are liberally interspersed with eating-houses and teashops. Dealers in tobacco, raisins, and cotton have a bazaar of their own, so have the traders in wool and camel's hair.

The covered bazaars of Bukhara, seen from above. In the centre: the cupola of the Goldsmiths' Bazaar

Almost every street in the bazaars terminates in the monumental building of some madrasah or mosque, whose cupola and façade are covered with gold or blue mosaics. The secret of making these coloured mosaics is lost, and they can nowadays be neither copied nor replaced. Even before the War Muslim piety had been un-availing to check a lively trade in these faiences with Russia and Persia; for European tourists will pay fabulous sums for them. The results of this collecting mania have been tragic in the extreme. The walls have been stripped of their lovely coverings up to the height of a man's outstretched arm and the laying bare of the brown mud which underlies these priceless tiles detracts enormously from the total effect. When you climb up and stand on one of the flat roofs from which the depredations of the vandals cannot be seen, the original effect is restored, and you are then most literally dazzled by the glory of blue and gold on every side. The unspoiled golden cupola of Gur i Shah, framed by the blue-tiled cupola and minarets of Diwan Begi, Khalifa Niaz, Harun ar Rashid, Mirza Ulugh Beg, Khiaban, Khalifa Hussain, Mir Arab, Madir Khan, and many others, constitute a sight which no one who has had the incalculable privilege of seeing it can ever forget.

The traffic in the streets of the city is indescribable. Caravans with heavily laden camels, high-piled carts, riders on horse and donkey, thrust through the narrow lanes and streets; Persians, Afghans, Indians, Tajiks, Chinese, Bukharan Jews, and representatives of dozens of other Asiatic peoples enliven the scene. Hindus, caste-mark on forehead, are chiefly busy as money-changers and actively compete in this business with the Parsees, who are at once distinguishable by their inky-black felt caps. The Afghans and Armenians are mainly moneylenders and still employ their ancient tally-sticks in preference to more modern methods of book-keeping. Woe to the dilatory debtor! If the day of reckoning passes with his debt still undischarged, the amount of it will infallibly be carved on the doorpost of his house, that every passer-by may know that he has been unable to meet his obligations.

The position of the Jews in Bukhara is unique. In earlier days they were considered unclean, and so much despised that they could not even be sold as slaves. They were forbidden to acquire land – they can do so less than ever now under the Soviet regime – and they were not allowed then or now to wear the gaily coloured robe or turban of Bukhara. In deference to the religious suscepti-bilities of their fellow citizens they are still compelled, as they have been for centuries, to wear a cap of felt or fur, to proclaim them unmistakably as Jews. They are forbidden to wear the Muslim sash round their waists and must close their cloaks with a narrow hempen cord. They are compelled to live in a special quarter of the city. Within the four walls of their own houses, however, they fling off coarse cap and cloak and wrap themselves in the magnificent garments and silken robes which are denied them without.

The silk merchants are mainly Afghans. They can at once be recognised by the little tail of cloth issuing from the folds of their turban and hanging coquettishly down over their left ear on to their breast. Amongst them you may occasionally see a modernised Bukharan woman. The ordinary woman's dress is still the loose robe or *paranja*, whose floating sleeves are tied together on the back, but the most vital item of her clothing, the *chimat* or horsehair veil, is nowadays frequently abandoned – not always to her advantage! The veil used mercifully to hide from view all kinds of uglinesses, and faces often devoured and scarred with skin disease, which is the terror of the Bukharan streets.

Bukhara possesses well over a hundred madrasahs (religious schools or universities) and remains still the centre of Islamic learning. You may here see the Red Star of the Soviet or the portraits of Lenin and Khidiralieff in queer juxtaposition with the ancient text-books of Shariat Law and commentaries on the Quran. The Madrasah Mir Arab is a typical example. The narrow cell of the Imam has shelves along the walls, laden with sacred books in Arabic and Kufic script, above which hangs a poster in Uzbeg which screams: 'Proletarians of all Lands Unite!' Few religious leaders in other parts of the world would be able to reconcile two philosophies so diametrically opposed. I ventured in some astonishment to ask how it was possible, and was informed that Bukharan students found no difficulty in keeping the teachings of Lenin and of Muhammad in two separate mental compartments.

Anti-God propaganda has had but little effect on the number of students attending the madrasahs. While I was in Bukhara 21,000 future mullas were receiving instruction in the city; they had journeyed from the remotest corners of Uzbegistan to study the teachings of the prophet of Islam. The teaching system of these schools or universities has not the faintest resemblance to ours. A verandah runs round the large central court, from which innumerable little doors lead into small windowless cells, whose sole furniture consists of a few felt rugs, a padded quilt, a comb, and a brass water-jug. When the hour of instruction comes, two or three pupils from the neighbouring cells gather in one of the tiny rooms and squat round their teacher on the ground, while he reads aloud in a chanting sing-song voice.

The largest building in Bukhara is the Citadel, the fortress of the last amirs, part of which has now been converted into an anti-imperial museum. The valuable sword which used to adorn the right-hand wing of the great entrance gate is no longer to be seen. The victorious Red troops carried it off to Tashkent, whence it disappeared in company with Ossipoff, and no trace of either has since been found. In compensation, as it were, the gigantic scourge, emblem of the might of the Amirs, which was formerly fixed on the other wing of the door, is now the chief show-piece of the museum. Chains, neck-rings, instruments of torture, executioners' swords and blocks, collected from all the prisons and dungeons of Bukhara, complete the contents of the museum. The pro-Communist psychological effect of the exhibits on the masses is undeniable.

Not far from the Citadel stands the Amir's summer castle, Shirbudun, with a half-European flavour about it. A tour of the extensive building is highly interesting. The apartments which were for the personal use of the Amir and his multitudinous wives have been preserved in their original state – like the Austrian castles of the Hapsburgs. With few exceptions, the walls of the rooms are simply colour-washed in white or grey. Large, almost modern windows open into the big gardens, once so rigorously secluded. The floors are tiled with stone or covered with mosaic. The lofty entrance door into the throne-room is magnificent. It is of carved rosewood and must be of immense value. The throne itself is only an outsize easy chair, whose broad arms did duty as a tea table. The

Amir had about twenty different bedrooms, now to one, now to another of which he constantly migrated in great secrecy as a precaution against assassination, just as his Turkish colleagues the Sultans of Constantinople were wont to do. The specially decorated bedroom in which he used to receive his favourite wife is probably the finest room in the castle. The walls are covered with heavy silken carpets, which nowadays, it must be admitted, have a somewhat shabby, threadbare look. The ceiling is of juniper and rosewood, the carving of which is said to have employed several artists over a period of thirty years. The floor is inlaid with beautifully preserved mosaic patterns in blue and gold.

The story goes that the grandfather of the last Amir, when he felt his end approaching, sent in haste for his favourite wife and three of his daughters and had them executed, so that no one else might touch or gaze on them after his death. For his own convenience he had the deed carried out beside his deathbed, so that he might see with his own eyes that his orders were obeyed.

The women's quarters are on the first floor. They show little to justify the wonderful descriptions which are often heard of the luxury of an oriental harem. They are simple and sober to a degree. But for the glorious silken carpets and the silk and damask coverings of the low bedsteads, you might think you were in a prison cell. Only a few rooms designed for special favourites are handsomely adorned; in them a ceiling of mirror glass reflects the few rays of light from a delicate rosewood lattice which are allowed to penetrate the darkness. But many things mysterious and romantic enough are here revealed. The guide stepped up to a large mirror in the wall. A touch on the hidden spring, and it moved aside, disclosing a secret stair. This leads to a large enclosed gallery surrounding a big hall. A number of small peepholes enable an observer to spy upon the scene below. While the women of his household were amusing themselves with games and dancing, the Amir would watch unseen by them, and make his choice. Another secret stair leads down from the gallery. At the bottom one passage leads into the hall and one to the Amir's private apartments. A

whole magazine of toys was piled in the women's hall: old gramo-
phones, dolls, mechanical figures, boxes of games, puppets like
those of our Punch and Judy shows, old French fashion journals,
picture books, and sets of building bricks had been collected to
minister to the amusement of the ladies.

In the opposite wing the guide opened the doors of a built-in
cupboard. A completely furnished railway sleeping-compartment
of the end of the nineteenth century came into view. The last
Amir's father had a passion for railway journeys and to indulge it
often travelled to and fro between Bukhara and Qaghan. The
mullas, however, objected, and he had an exact copy made of a
sleeping compartment. Behind the window of the compartment
there was a tiny room in which his servants used to stand and wave
strips of coloured paper past the window panes so that His Majesty
might enjoy the complete illusion of a railway journey.

The next room was fitted out as a small private mosque. The six
chandeliers with which it was lighted up are of solid gold – or were
up till 1920. Next to this is the ladies' bath. A large tiled basin served
as a swimming bath, the water of which was heated by the simple
device of lighting a big fire in the cellar below. Individual bathtubs
of copper or zinc were ranged all round the walls; dented and full
of holes as they now are, they give the place an air of desolation.
About nine feet from the ground there are barred windows of red
glass which shed a rosy light into the bathing room. A neighbouring
room is provided with peepholes, through which again the Amir
could secretly observe his women while they bathed.

From the bath the guide led me into the so-called Labyrinth, a
large octagonal hall which is divided by partitions into the sem-
blance of a maze. Here the Amir used to play at chasing the beauties
whom he had selected from the bath. If report speaks true it was
the dream of every inmate of the harem to hear the eunuch's
summons to the Labyrinth – because every opportunity of intimacy
with the Amir spelt jewels and privileges, and might prove the first
step towards the coveted position of favourite.

The guide of the museum was the man who had been the last

head eunuch of the Court. He had betrayed the secret hiding-places and treasure houses to the Red troops. His knowledge of the castle led to the discovery of the many concealed passages, stairs, and trap-doors, and also of the Amir's secret prison, whose existence had always been denied. When the Red soldiers took possession of

Tank in garden of my dwelling house in Bukhara. Left: back view of the Harun ar Rashid Mosque

the Citadel and opened the secret dungeons they set free eighteen imprisoned men and women, chiefly sons and daughters of the Amir, but also some Court dignitaries who had mysteriously disappeared.

The Russian and Bukharan Bolsheviks naturally made capital out of these revelations. They took the trouble to bring in as many nomads and peasants from the oases as possible, to demonstrate effectively to them the habits and cruelties of their former Amir.

From Shirbudun to the Citadel there runs an underground passage by which the Amir made his escape in 1920.

One must give the Bolsheviks their due. They have reformed

and modernised the army – their main support in Bukhara – from top to bottom. I had been twice on a long visit to Bukhara in 1919 and I had had opportunity to inform myself about the equipment and training of the Bukharan Army of those days, and to observe various military manoeuvres and exercises outside the city gates. The soldiers' uniform was a dark-blue tunic with enormously wide red trousers which fell in great folds over their battered knee-boots. They wore black lambskin caps on their heads with brass badges displaying the arms of the Amir – a hand with outspread fingers – and the arms of the country, a crescent and a star. Their weapons were a curved sabre, often innocent of scabbard, and an antique Russian gun with incredibly long bayonet. Even the Amir's guard before the palace often went on duty with torn uniforms and in summer often barefoot. Unwashed, unshaven, patched, and ragged, with miscellaneous odds and ends of uniform, they presented the most miserable and neglected appearance. The cavalry on their small shaggy steppe ponies looked if possible even worse. The Bukharan Army had a few lines of artillery, too, such as you may occasionally see in museums at home. These muzzle-loaders were cast in brass and inscribed with cabalistic and magic formulae, and their throats terminated in terrifying snakes and dragons' heads. At the very time of which I write there was in Ab i Garm a great store of machine-guns and modern breech-loaders, not to mention magazine rifles and automatic pistols. If the Amir had armed his men with these weapons in good time, who knows? He might still have been master of the country.

The Soviets have equipped the modern Red Army of Bukhara with the very latest of modern weapons and trained them in their use. Gone are the full beards dyed with henna. Fine, healthy, upstanding figures, dressed in light brown khaki, drill and exercise with admirable precision. The little ponies of the steppes have been replaced by excellent Turkoman horses, and a corps of camelry is responsible for desert service.

The great bazaar square covers about half a square mile in front of the Citadel. Hundreds of tiny booths surround the open square in the midst of which lies the largest of Bukhara's many *hauz* or open tanks of water, bounded on the north and west by two madrasahs, and on the east by the New Prison. The German, Count Schweinitz, who stayed in Bukhara in 1910 – the last European to visit the city before the World War – declared that this prison was most admirable and that all the yarns about the ghastly prison conditions of Bukhara were untrue. The good count was bamboozled by the wily Bukharans; they showed him only the prison reserved for such high officials and dignitaries, relatives, and ex-favourites of the Amir as had begun to prove a trifle inconvenient. This explains how the count could say that he had seen only four cells housing in all some twenty prisoners. They took good care not to show him the dungeons of Zindan and Khaudan, in which hundreds of poor devils festered away in underground holes, and in which many European prisoners, including the Englishmen Conolly and Stoddart, were incarcerated until their execution. Nowadays the old prisons have been abolished and the comparatively luxurious prison of the big officials is used for ordinary criminals, while political prisoners are dispatched to Moscow or Tashkent.

If you climb up one of the many minarets of Bukhara you see below an almost uniform mud roof, dotted with occasional large or smaller swellings. There are few open lanes or streets passing through the centre of the town; most of them are roofed over, and it is possible to walk from end to end of the city on the continuous roofs of houses and streets.

Between the Mosque of Kalan and the Mir Arab Madrasah rises the tall minaret of the Mir Arab, known as the 'Tower of Death'. Under the rule of the Amirs condemned criminals were sewn up in sacks and flung down from this minaret. They crashed on to the stone pavement, and were left lying there.

A few years before the Great War the Amir, in deference to the wishes of the Tsar, gave up this method of execution and adopted that of cutting people's heads off. After the War had begun, however, and Bukhara's independence was re-established, the slinging of people from the minaret was resumed as a regular part of the legal procedure of the Amirate.

One of the saddest corners of Bukhara is the Lepers' Quarter. It has nothing on the outside to distinguish it, nor is it barred from the inside. Here in some hundreds of wretched mud huts these unfortunates live and beget children, doomed all their lives to see nothing of the world but the miserable hovels of the lepers. Every inhabitant of Bukhara has the right to slay at sight any leper whom he sees outside the quarter. Now, under the rule of the Soviets, these unhappy people are cared for by the State, whereas they were formerly abandoned to the charity of their relations or of any chance benefactor. Many of those interned in the Lepers' Quarter are not suffering from leprosy at all; but medical knowledge being very elementary, any one unlucky enough to develop a white patch on any visible portion of the skin is immediately banished there. Artists in cosmetics who have skill enough to restore such white patches to a normal appearance are therefore in great demand and earn enormous fees.

The cemeteries of Bukhara are curiously laid out. The majority of them are most unhygienically situated inside the city walls. At first, for strategic reasons, houses used to be built at some distance from the city wall, but during the last twenty years less thought was given to strategy and a great number of mud houses have been built right up against the inner side of it, interspersed with frequent graveyards. The inhabitants of Central Asia, including Bukhara, bury their dead differently from us. The corpse is not sunk underground, but a mud platform is built up, twelve or fifteen inches high, and a barrel-shaped wall is vaulted over it. The back is closed in first, leaving the front open. Then the corpse is pushed into the low vault and the front built up, leaving open a small square hole. A burial usually takes place within twelve or fifteen hours of death, while according to the people's religious belief the soul requires at least three days to extricate itself from the body. The hole is therefore necessary to let the soul escape and make its way

The oldest story-teller in Bukhara. He had been a Court singer to three
successive Khans of Khiwa, and finally had been in the service of the Amir
of Bukhara

179

to Paradise, and every grave is conscientiously supplied with this outlet. A little oil-lamp is placed in the hole, and must be lighted on the third, seventh, and fourteenth day. At the same time flaps of bread cooked in fat are also placed in the hole to provide the soul with food for its journey. Not the soul alone, but all the gases of decomposition issue from this opening, while cats and dogs creep in and drag out pieces of the decaying flesh, which are left lying about. No Believer would venture to touch any part of a dead body, for fear of preventing its owner from reaching Paradise.

The space available for burial grounds in Bukhara is very restricted, so the grave-mounds are not ranged side by side or one behind the other, but built up over each other many stories high, so that the graveyard ultimately looks like a gigantic honeycomb. The pressure of the upper graves and the weathering of the mud vaults often break down the vaults of the lower graves, which naturally causes the collapse of the top ones and the release of skeletons and decaying bodies. The winter rains help the work of destruction, and it is not at all rare to see skeletons and half-rotted corpses lying about amongst the crumbling graves.

In spite of all this, health conditions in Bukhara are not so unfavourable as might be expected. Apart from the *rishta*, or guinea-worm, which I have described in the first chapter of this book, the most frequently occurring illness is the *pendinka*, a kind of septic ulcer which usually attacks face, neck, and hands, and leaves the most unsightly scars behind. Another very prevalent disease is the so-called 'Blue Sickness'. The skin of the sufferer becomes dry and brittle and comes away from the body in tatters, but without falling off completely. This disease resembles an extremely severe attack of sunburn, except that it attacks the entire skin and causes the most intense pain, while the skin turns almost blue. The unfortunate victims have to go without clothing for months and can neither lie nor sit, since the slightest pressure is agony. The cause of the Blue Sickness is unknown, and there is no known treatment for it. In addition to these complaints, leprosy and venereal disease have their victims.

In spite of the vileness of the water-supply, typhus and typhoid are of rare occurrence. The water-supply consists of some eighty large *hauz* or ponds situated in different parts of the city, from which the different quarters are supplied by open canals or *ariqs*. Thousands and thousands of frogs and toads flourish in these *hauz* and *ariqs*, dead dogs and cats float about in them, and every earthly kind of refuse is thrown into them. Milliards of worms and water fleas also populate the water reservoirs and canals, from which all cooking and washing water is drawn. Dogs, donkeys, and horses bathe in them; sick and well alike wash face, feet, and hands in them. I once saw a man with a *pendinka* washing his face, which was covered with suppurating boils, in one of these *hauz*, and for days after I could not bring myself to drink tea or eat any food cooked in water.

And yet those ponds of Bukhara are wonderfully beautiful. In the evening, after the muezzin has sounded from the minaret the Call to Prayer, the men of the city gather round the ponds, which are bordered by tall silver poplars and magnificent black elms, to enjoy a period of ease and leisure. Carpets are spread, the ever-burning *chilim* is passed from mouth to mouth, the samovar steams away, and lightfooted boys hand round the shallow bowls of green tea. Here the *meddahs*, or story-tellers, the musicians, and the dancing boys assemble to display their craft. And perhaps a conjuror or a juggler comes, performing the most amazing and incredible feats of skill. An Indian snake-charmer joins the throng and sets his poisonous snakes to dance, while over all reigns the peace of a Bukharan evening. No loud speech breaks the spell; items of scandal and the news of the day are exchanged in discreet whispers. So it was centuries ago in Bukhara; so it is today. There are things which not even the Soviets can alter.

XIII

The Domain of the Amu Darya

I travelled southwards by train in the direction of Charjui, alighted at Farab, and waited there for a caravan which was starting for Patta Kasar, and accompanied it as far as Burdaliq. The caravan road runs through the broad green belt of the Amu Darya to the south-west of Bukhara. The thick jungle of reeds is broken by miserable little *qishlaqs*. These villages ingeniously use the marshy stretches of land for the cultivation of rice. At times the road follows the raised line of a lofty shifting sand-dune, which permits an extensive view over the great desert that stretches on both sides of the river. Though the land near the river is extremely fertile it is sparsely inhabited, a fact which is probably to be explained by the high mortality from malaria and marsh fever. The little villages seldom boast even the usual huts. They mainly consist of low, primitive reed hovels, roughly plastered on the outside with mud. As far as Narazim the population is predominantly Turkoman, while between Narazim and Hazrat Bashir it is Qirghiz with a strong admixture of Uzbeg.

We pitched our last camp one night not far from Iska. While the men were busy feeding the animals and cooking the evening meal the caravan-*bashi* called me to come with him, he had something interesting to show me. He twisted bundles of reeds into rude torches and by their light he led me up a loess hill till we reached a large hole like a door in a mud wall. As long as the torches held out he guided me through a labyrinth of passages and caves which appeared to stretch several miles under the ground. We saw old hearths, broken pots, weapons, and metal utensils eaten by rust,

182

all of which must have been very old, and lots of animal bones, often piled up in layers. As I have already mentioned, there are many such underground cities in Turkistan which have not been inhabited in recent times. Not a single cave had fallen in or become impassable. Loess is such a firm and durable earth that everything was in a perfect state of preservation, as if these caves had been but newly excavated. I was sceptical of the great age he attributed to this city of caves till I talked to a Balti doctor in Charjui who had visited and explored almost all the Turkoman cave-dwellings in the country. He believed the caves to be ancient centres of civilisation and was of the opinion that they would be found to contain much valuable archaeological material if they were made accessible to scientists. So far, he deplored, the Russian Government had paid almost no heed to their existence.

When we scrambled back to camp we found that a lot of very smoky fires, fed with reeds and green wood, had been lit round the tents in an attempt to drive off the swarms of mosquitos. It must be confessed that they were entirely useless for the purpose. Whole clouds of these blood-sucking malaria-carriers flung themselves on men and animals. I at once took a double dose of quinine and persevered with this precaution as long as we remained in the Amu Darya neighbourhood. Neither Europeans nor natives use mosquito nets in Turkistan or take any prophylactic measures against malaria. Whoever is attacked just passively endures and perishes – Insha' Allah, if God will.

I took my bedding and dragged it off some distance into the cave, which none of the mosquitos appeared to have invaded. As soon as I had assured myself of this welcome fact, I returned to camp with the good news, expecting that it would be greeted with joy. The *bashi* assured me that he had known it for years, but that they were all in God's hands and didn't care a fig for mosquito bites. So I left my friends to be bitten to death and duly infected with malaria, while I returned to sleep by myself in the cave.

The land dips between Iska and Narazim and is thus one of the few spots in Bukhara that can be watered directly from the Amu

Darya, for the rest of the country lies definitely above the river. Innumerable canals greatly impeded our progress, for according to their depth we had either to wade or swim across. This caravan road along the Amu Darya must be one of the oldest in the world, but it cannot boast a single bridge. Some of the smaller canals were only a couple of yards wide and two feet or so deep, but the large ones ran to a width of five or six yards and a depth of over six feet.

It was fun to watch the Turkomans when it came to crossing these canals: at any time they love water about as much as a cat. Before we came to the first big one we had crossed perhaps a score of smaller. Men and animals had simply plunged into the thick, opaque mud-water and forded through it. This time the matter was not so simple. The stream was a good six yards wide and was rushing downhill with considerable force. The caravan came to a halt. Some people took sheep-skins from their saddles and began to blow them up by one leg. Gradually the skins filled, the tied legs stuck stiffly out, and soon the whole thing looked like a fat, unshaven pig. Then the men stripped, climbed down the bank to the edge of the water, laid the inflated skin across their chest, and swimming with both hands, successfully landed on the farther bank.

These same *tursuq* were used by Chinghiz Khan and Tamerlane for crossing rivers. In the desert the skins serve to carry the water-supply, and when you come to a river they offer you a boat. When flaying the carcass of a sheep such skins as are destined for these purposes are not slit down the belly, but carefully drawn off in one piece; the openings at foot and neck are tied with thongs while still wet, so that the skin is made both air- and water-tight. When you want to fill or blow them up, you can open either a neck or leg hole and firmly lash it again afterwards.

It took us hours to coax the water-shy camels through the water, so that we could only accomplish a march of three tash that day. The numerous skins were not deflated, but taken along blown out as they were, so as to be immediately ready for the next crossing. The Turkomans had, however, omitted to reckon with the expansion of air under the heat of the sun, and before long one float after another burst with a loud report, and when we came to the next wide canal the skins had all to be patched before they could be used again. All these delays made our progress so slow that we did not reach Narazim till the afternoon of the third day, though the distance from Charjui is well under sixty miles.

In its day, Narazim was a great fortress, which the Bukharans had erected for their defence against the Turkomans, and during the War it was the headquarters of a large Russian garrison. Nowadays it is a place of no strategic importance, and its former barracks have either fallen into decay or been turned into storehouses for saksaul. But it is still the centre of a lively caravan traffic with the interior of Bukhara, for no district in the whole of Turkistan is richer than the neighbourhood of Narazim in the valuable saksaul. Although tens of thousands of camel-loads are dug up and dispatched every year, the supply seems inexhaustible. There is not much of it to be seen immediately near the river, for boatloads of it are carried off downstream year in year out, and the ships themselves use saksaul as fuel, so you must ride some miles inland into the desert to see regular forests of this curious tree.

The saksaul-tree – known to science as *Haloxylon ammodendron* – is only found in the salt-impregnated sand deserts of the Amu Darya and the Sir Darya, and grows under the ground, or, more exactly, under the sand. Its black or dark-brown wood is extremely hard, yet it splinters and breaks like glass, the fracture revealing a surface like artificial horn or solidified rubber. It is heavier than water and even when perfectly dry sinks like a stone. It is of no use except for fuel, for it cannot be either cut or planed. Carvings in saksaul are of the greatest rarity and literally worth their weight in gold. The only ones of any size that I have seen were in a mausoleum in the neighbourhood of Bukhara. The gnarled and many-branched trunk grows to a length of over thirty feet, and usually lies buried ten or twelve inches deep in the sand. It grows with many twists and turns and where parts of the stem come to the surface it suggests a gigantic snake in movement. A cross-section of the trunk shows a sort of flattened ellipse. Thin little twigs with tiny, almost invisible leaves shoot up from the exposed portions of the trunk; the leaves are ashen grey and snuggle so close to the twigs that they are scarcely visible with the naked eye. When the wood is burned it gives off spicy, fragrant fumes which produce a kind of intoxication. The ash remaining is pure and white like snow and is used by the natives both as a medicine and as a disinfectant. The tree takes a hundred and fifty years to reach its maximum development, and the full-sized trunk is then thirteen or fourteen inches in diameter.

After Narazim we took a ford across the river, which is here nearly a mile wide, because the right bank, up almost as far as Burdaliq, is one immense swamp which is most tedious and wearying to travel through. The sandbanks and fords of the Amu are perpetually changing their position, so the guide we had engaged in Narazim crossed the river first by himself to explore the route. The water frequently reached his chin, but having got safely over he returned and piloted the whole caravan to the other side without a single casualty. At this point the left bank lies again in Turkoman territory, and is one of the most fertile stretches in the whole course of the river. The cultivated area, where cotton and cornfields succeed each other without a break, is only a few miles wide, and then merges into the southern Qara Qum.

Late in the evening we reached Talliq, a little place directly opposite Islam, whose occasional lights were reflected in the water. As it would have been folly to attempt a second crossing of the great river at night, we were obliged to camp in Talliq. Next morning, escorted by local guides, we crossed once more to the right bank and rode back the five miles or so into Burdaliq. Some Qirghiz had pitched their yurts between the fortress and the river and I now got the chance to see them training eagles and falcons for the chase.

Burdaliq, which up to 1920 was a great Bukharan fortress, possesses high defensive walls, whose towers and parapets are still in as good a state of preservation as if they had been built a few months ago. The place is still one of the most important caravan junctions of Turkistan. Desert tracks radiate in all directions, and on the one hand connect the most southerly quarters of Turkistan with central and eastern Bukhara, and on the other the north-west and the north-east of Afghanistan with Turkistan. As befits their importance the bazaars and serais are extensive, very nearly equalling those of Bukhara itself. Lively business and traffic fill the narrow lanes of Burdaliq, which seems so far as little affected by the teachings of Communism as by its efforts to restrict production and regulate barter. Red flags and pictures of Lenin are rare curiosities, and it seems as if the prehistoric traditions of Bukhara had taken refuge here. All day long caravans were coming in from every quarter, but mainly from Afghanistan, richly laden with wares of every kind, and the short road that stretches from Islam to Burdaliq, which lies a trifle off the main route, was thronged from morning to night with busy animals and men. Never before had I been so much struck by the gay colours of men's robes, the dreary look of veiled women, and the briskness of bazaar life as I was here. Possibly the impression was heightened by the narrowness of lanes and bazaars, but it was certainly very strong.

Again I made the round of all the caravanserais, seeking news of a caravan that would be travelling by the Four Wells route to Yolatan on the Murgh Ab railway. With so much business doing, my task was easy and I had soon struck a bargain with some Turkomans who owned a lot of transport camels. Four hundred camels, laden with charcoal, which had already been eleven days on the road, were going to start in a short time on the second half of their journey to Takhta Bazaar, and I proposed to join their company. The road from Burdaliq to Yolatan runs through some hundred and fifty miles of the south-eastern Qara Qum, in which there is neither plant nor human habitation. Nothing but the existence of four wells – Kulach, Imirsti, Jarjik, and Daali – make it possible to cross the desert of gravel. This part of the Qara Qum no longer consists of sand, but is for the most part composed of coarse gravel and patches of hard salt. It lacks even the miserable vegetation that is sparsely scattered throughout the sand desert.

Once more, and as it happened for the last time, I crossed the Amu Darya and bade farewell to its waters. Though it was only four days since we had last forded it, the water had perceptibly fallen, and we were able to wade in comfort from one island to another. We filled all our water-skins in Talliq and committed ourselves to the mercy of the desert. Though this part of the Qara Qum is exceptionally rich in salt we were pleasantly surprised to find that the deep wells yielded unexpectedly sweet drinking water. The last salt lakes must but recently have dried out, for the heavily laden camels frequently broke through the surface crust of salt and sank into the mud below.

The storms of the Black Desert are deservedly feared, but on this occasion we had the good fortune completely to escape them. The frequent lengthy wind-storms must be the cause of the desert-floor's being swept completely bare of sand and left covered only with heavy gravel, while in the course of centuries the fine surface sand has been swept off westwards and there banked up. Storms always blow from the south-east, down from the mountains of Afghanistan, north-westwards up into the centre of the Qara Qum.

Never, either before or since, have I seen anything so desolate and dead as this gravel desert. Not even the unexacting camel-thorn or the saksaul is to be seen, and except round the wells there is not a bush, not a blade of grass. Even animal life is absent. Except for our own donkeys and camels I saw not a quadruped or bird or reptile, in which Turkistan elsewhere is rich enough. There was not even a beetle or a worm. The very horseflies had quitted our animals in Talliq and remained by the waters of the Amu – much to the beasts' content, for they had been suffering sorely from the attentions of these blood-suckers.

On the fifth day after our start from Burdaliq we reached the oasis of Yolatan on the Murgh Ab. This was the place I had reached on foot by night when I escaped from Merv in 1916. The caravan now continued upstream along the Murgh Ab, while I waited for a train to Merv, which I reached by rail in a few hours.

This brought me back to the starting-point of my Bukharan

journey, which had led me a round 5,600 miles through mountain and desert. To be candid, I had by now had more than enough, and my craving for adventure had for the moment been amply satisfied. I felt homesick for my peaceful life in Persia, for my carpet-buying journeys, and I dreamt of a return to my home in Vienna at no distant date.

XIV

How to Get Out?

I had managed without too much difficulty to make my way into the forbidden land. But how was I to get safely out again? The simplest plan would have been to travel back to Qizil Arwat, join Alim Qul and his tribe, and return to Persia by the way I had come. But I dare not venture on the journey between Aidin and Qala Qaya, across the waterless Khambaghi Qum, without a guide. Khores had told me often enough that no caravans ever went that way and that only people knowing the desert thoroughly had any chance of getting through in safety. There was not the slightest hope that I, without a camel and water-skins, could safely risk a journey which even the Turkoman sons of the desert think twice about. My funds were so low that I could not afford to buy either a camel or the necessary equipment. This line of retreat was therefore cut off, for I had no means of communicating with Alim Qul and asking him to let some one fetch me from Aidin.

The only other course possible was somehow to sneak across the frontier in the strongly guarded district between Dushak and Ashqabad. As to exactly how it was to be done, my plans could only be improvised on the spot according to time and circumstance. I took a ticket to Dushak, from which there is a caravan route across the frontier mountains to Kalat and Darband. If it was not possible to get over somewhere in this direction I must just take my chance at Lutfabad and aim at reaching Imam Gah, or else aim at getting from Ashqabad to Shirwan. Whichever route I decided on I should need to take every precaution not to be collared by Soviet troops on the border. What made the business peculiarly dangerous was

190

that a decree was posted up everywhere, forbidding any one whomsoever, on any pretext whatsoever, to approach within six and a half miles of the frontier. Frontier posts were instructed to shoot at sight anyone attempting to contravene the order.

I made cautious inquiries in Dushak and learnt that all the frontier passes were well watched and garrisoned, for this was the chief line of communication with north-east Persia. So I went on by rail to Nurak and took up my quarters in the only *chai-khana* in the place. I gradually succeeded in winning the confidence of the *chai-khana-chik*, and after some questioning I told him that I wanted a guide to smuggle me by unfrequented by-paths into Persia. For many years the Turkomans, when not occupied in raiding, have carried on a brisk smuggling business. Knowledge of secret tracks is inherited from father to son, and one fine evening I found myself seated opposite the eighteen-year-old scion of a trusty smuggler-dynasty. Our negotiations lasted for hours, till at last we had fixed a price, in return for which the promising youth undertook to land me safely across the border.

In addition to sixty roubles in cash I was to hand him over my watch, my shaving gear, and compass, and also my rifle – which it is true was strictly the property of the Uzbeg Soviet and had been only lent to me. But I did not indulge any qualms of conscience on this score. In any case I dare not take it with me, for it would have been far too dangerous to be caught with firearms near the frontier. My guide was to get the watch, rifle, etc., before we started, and the cash as soon as we were safely over the border. I sewed my pistol and a few cartridges into my thick quilted coat in such a way that the weapon lay under my armpit. I similarly sewed my Persian passport into the leg of one of my long boots. I burnt all my notes and other papers except the genuine Steinschneider document and my permit from the Samarqand Soviet.

The day before I meant to leave, the devil of over-confidence took possession of me and I addressed one of the picture postcards which I had bought in Merv to the Russian consul in Enzeli who had forbidden me to attempt to enter Turkistan. Then I put

Steinschneider's paper in an envelope and posted it and the card in the mail waggon of the passing train, for I could not face the double journey of 250 miles to Qizil Arwat and back to deliver the paper in person. My camera, films, and other scanty possessions I then packed in a small *khurjin* or saddlebag.

My guide duly turned up on the morning of the 26th of August 1925; we mounted our donkeys and turned them back in the direction of Dushak. We followed the railway line at first till we came to the little Kalat river whose bed at this season was completely dry, then we rode up the empty river-bed for a couple of hours. At last my guide called a halt and we lay down under some half-withered mulberry trees to sleep, so as to be fresh for our night adventure. At the first streak of dawn we climbed and climbed up a steep mountain side covered with loose stones. So far we had not seen a trace of any path or track. According to the guide we were nearly two miles away from the nearest road, so that there was no fear of our being discovered. We sought shelter from the sun under an overhanging rock, allowed ourselves a gulp of water and a few flaps of dry bread, and sank into a sleep of exhaustion.

Towards noon, when the sun was at its highest, I woke up and automatically stretched out for the sheepskin to quench my thirst. The movement roused my companion. He snatched the skin from my lips and explained that our drinking supply had to last us for two days if we were not to perish of thirst. So I pulled my little pebbles from my pocket and offered him one. As so often before, they greatly helped to mitigate our thirst.

The youth told me that the first three ridges of the Kupat Dagh have only one spring amongst them. In springtime, when the snows begin to melt, there are plenty of little torrents and pools of snow-water, but all moisture has evaporated again by April. Like a great wall the mountains cut Persia off from the Qara Qum. From the Caspian Sea to the Afghan frontier – a good six hundred miles – the Kupat Dagh and its outliers form a natural barrier between Persia and Turkistan. The mountains rise steeply from the desert of sand and there are very few traversable passes, a fact which makes this long frontier comparatively easy to guard. There are in all only six passes through which the roads are possible for men and beasts. Since the Soviets assumed power three of these have been permanently closed and only the Kifan, Firuza, and Lutfabad left available for traffic. Naturally there are dozens of secret tracks, but they are known only to smugglers and it needs courage to cross them, for they run through waterless, rocky desert, and involve serious mountaineering feats. So much so, that in fact it often happens that out of a smuggling gang only a small number, or none, return.

The view which we had from our first halting-place in the mountains was overwhelming. To north and east and west the great Qara Qum stretched out into infinity. Not a patch of green broke the uniform grey-yellow surface which blended into the distant horizon. But for the darker lines of the dunes you would have imagined you were looking down on an immense sheet of glass strewn with sand. Though I was looking at only a small fraction of the great desert I got some conception of its immensity; it covers about 75,000 square miles – roughly two and a half times the area of Austria, or of Scotland.

Night came again, and we continued our climb. My guide must have known the country like the palm of his hand, for he never halted nor hesitated but continued to climb straight up. I followed as closely as I could, so as not to lose him in the darkness. The moon presently rose, and by her light I was able to make out that we were crossing a lofty plateau covered with great boulders and broken rocks, but otherwise completely bare. About midnight we halted for a rest. The Turkoman bade me lie quietly where I was while he went to fetch water from the spring near at hand. An hour passed and I was getting anxious, wondering whether he had left me in the lurch and was perhaps already well on the way home to Nurak. Just then he returned with a sheepskin full of fresh water, which I greedily drank.

The night was distinctly chilly, and, newly refreshed, we stepped out more briskly to warm our stiffened limbs. The high plateau now gave way to a steep gorge, along the bottom of which we tramped downhill. According to my Turkoman, we had one more mountain ridge to climb and we should then have reached our highest point, some 9,000 feet above sea-level. I felt completely secure, and after having been assured by the guide that there was not the slightest danger, I lit myself a cigarette. It had just caught, and I was in the act of flinging away the still burning match, when the youth pulled me to the ground beside him and at the same moment I heard a voice: 'Halt! Who goes there?' Even if my companion had not put his hand over my mouth I should not have been able to answer, so terrified and surprised was I by the sudden challenge. With one leap the Turkoman was on his feet and had vanished into the darkness. Simultaneously I saw a flash within a few yards of me, a shot rang out and struck sparks out of the stone before me, then other shots followed my fleeing guide. I lay low, as still as death, till I heard the invisible marksman say: 'Stand up!' I rose obediently and held up my hands.

'Who are you?'

'A state geologist of the Uzbeg Soviet.'

'Have you got papers?'

'Of course,' said I, and made to take them from my pocket.

'Halt! Hands up! Why have you run away?'

'You can see that I haven't run away. My friend fled because he thought you were a bandit.'

'Where have you come from?'

'From Merv.'

'Lie down. No, not like that, flat on your face. If you turn I'll shoot. Make no mistake about it.'

I lay down on the ground as he bade me. He put his rifle behind a stone and drew his pistol. Then he knelt on my back, and while with one hand he pressed the pistol against the back of my head, he tried to rummage through my pockets with the other. At last he found the grubby, well-thumbed document of the Soviet of Samarqand. He shoved a box of matches into my hand and made me strike one after another until he had deciphered the paper. Then he let me stand up again and keep my hands down.

'I'm awfully sorry, Comrade,' he said, 'but I must take you along with me to the frontier post. We have had no notification to say you were authorised to do geology in the frontier zone. So come quietly. If you try to resist, it is my duty to shoot.'

I stood up and went in the direction indicated, while the soldier kept close on my heels and shouted instructions as to which way I was to turn. By degrees I had mastered the first shock, and was racking my brains for some method of escape. After about an hour's marching we were up again on the high plateau. My guide and I had come from the north; my captor now led me due east. I begged that we might have a short halt. The soldier didn't mind, he sat down a few paces off, but never for a moment left his rifle out of his hand. I flung him a couple of cigarettes, which he gratefully accepted, and we smoked in silence for half an hour or so. Then we started off again.

Quarter of an hour later I gave a cry of pain and fell to the ground. My captor asked what had happened. I said I had slipped on a stone and thought I must have broken my ankle. I seemed to have damaged my arm too in the fall, for I found I could not move it. The soldier sat down near me and seemed to be thinking what his next move ought to be. Such a contingency was apparently not foreseen in the textbooks of the Red Army.

I groaned with pain, and begged a drink of water. The soldier knelt beside me and held his water-bottle to my lips. I drank slowly and in little sips. Slowly and unobtrusively I raised my right hand till I felt the hilt of his pistol. With one wrench I snatched it from his belt and held it in a flash against his breast with a cry of 'Hands up!' while the contents of his drinking-flask poured over my face.

'Now, my son, just you lie down nicely on your face and put your hands behind your back.'

Without a word he complied with my wishes. In frontier encounters there is no room for argument. Death is prompter than speech. Besides, my surprise attack had so completely taken his breath away that he didn't think of resisting. I first made his hands fast with the belt of my trousers so that he could not use them.

Then I turned him over and helped him to sit up. When he was comfortably seated, his first words were: 'Then you didn't break your ankle after all?'

'No, my son. Now listen! If you'll take me safely across the frontier into Persia, not a thing shall happen to you, and you shall return to your post safe and sound. If you refuse, or if I think you are trying to betray me, I shall shoot you down on the instant. You can take my word for it that I am dead in earnest.'

I now began to search the fellow. Apart from a few roubles, a packet of tobacco, and a bundle of paper for twisting into little holders to smoke it in, he had nothing in his pockets. His haversack contained a little dried meat and a few rifle cartridges. I left him all his things, subtracting only the Caucasian dagger from his belt. Then I took his rifle, and in exchange loaded my saddlebag and the half-empty water-skin on to his shoulders. We now set out for Persia with roles reversed. At his request I unstrapped his hands during the march. When we retired into a cave at dawn to pass the day there I tied him up hands and feet so as to be able to sleep in peace myself. Then I fed him with his own dried meat, of which he genially offered me the half.

Before we were ready to start out again that night we were chatting happily together like old friends. My prisoner told me that for the last few years every one who wanted to leave Russia secretly chose the Persian in preference to the Russo-Rumanian border, because the latter was now so well guarded that there was no hope of slipping across the Dniester, whether over the ice in winter or in summer by boat. It happened almost daily that some would-be fugitives fell to Russian bullets on the Dniester, some even after they had reached the Rumanian bank. Moscow reckons the total number of those who previously escaped across the Dniester at round about a million and a half, while so far not more than about 200,000 have succeeded in crossing into Persia. The Persian frontiers are now being carefully watched to make this route also impracticable. Hence the guards' instructions to fire at sight.

This time we ventured to start our march while it was still

daylight, for the soldier maintained that we had already left the Russian guard-houses well behind us, and that in fact when he had arrested me we had actually been on Persian soil. When it got quite dark we halted on the southern slope of the second range to wait for morning. I again tied my guide up and built a three-foot wall of stones, behind which I ventured to light a fire and make tea for us both, with which we ate the last of his meat. My absolutely last remaining iron ration was two pounds or so of dried apricot. After our modest supper I assured myself that my companion could not free himself, rolled over in my robe, and went to sleep.

I was wakened by kicks on my leg, and leaped up, afraid that my prisoner had managed to free himself after all. But there he was all right, and only raised his head to listen. He whispered that he had wakened me because he had heard footsteps. I listened too. It certainly seemed that several people must be making their way over the loose stones, for we could distinctly hear the shuffling sound of shoes and the rattling of stones. I crept over to Vassili Andreyvich, put my lips close to his ear, and asked who he thought the night wanderers could be. He replied that it must either be smugglers or else Persian gendarmes out on a smuggler hunt; in either case we had better lie low. The night was still and for a long time we continued to hear the sounds growing steadily more distant. Day broke soon after they had ceased and we resumed our way, turning down the valley. We passed a little cave, where I hid the soldier's rifle and pistol along with his cartridges, so that he could pick them up on his way back to duty. He would just have to explain his lengthy absence as best he could. Then I took off my *khilat* and under the astonished gaze of Vassili Andreyvich I ripped open the place where I had stowed my Browning. For safety I shoved a set of cartridges into the magazine and put the loaded weapon in my pocket ready for use.

Towards midday we saw far below us a fairly well-made road, along which some armed horsemen were riding at the trot. The Russian diagnosed them as Persian gendarmes. I then pulled off my long-boot and took my Persian passport out of the leg, while I tore my document of the Samarqand Soviet into tiny fragments and scattered them to the winds. If the Persians were to find it on me they might suspect me of being a Bolshevik agent. I then restored to Vassili Andreyvich his freedom. He assured me that now that he had got to know me he would have been very sorry if he had handed me over to the frontier post. As a reward for his services as guide and in payment for the Caucasian dagger I gave him the half of my remaining cash, namely thirty roubles, for which he thanked me with genuine and effusive gratitude. I for my part apologised most heartily for having had to use trickery and force against him. Whereupon we parted the best of friends.

After a lot of handshaking and repetitions of 'Au revoir, Comrade', I climbed down the scree into the valley and tramped along the road in the direction of Marish. By the afternoon I had scaled the third mountain ridge and had, by an excellent road, reached the blooming and fertile valley beyond, with the fourth ridge still ahead of me. I soon came into a small, delightfully clean village surrounded by high walls. I went to the headman of the village and introduced myself as a buyer of carpets. The man laughed me to scorn for being such a fool as to look for carpets in the Kupat Dagh. I had achieved my purpose, however, for the hospitable fellow invited me to spend the night as his guest. Next morning he put a horse at my disposal and sent a gendarme with me to the next village to bring the horse back. Profiting by this experience, I repeated the same experiment in every place I came to, which greatly aided my progress and saved me the cost of my keep. In this wise I crossed the fifth and last ridge of the mountains at the foot of which lies the village of Quchan. Here I came once more into the kingdom of rich ricefields and slender silver poplar. The method of irrigation used on the southern slopes of the Kupat Dagh was new to me. The water of the mountain springs is collected and led by underground canals, called *karéz*[1] to the fields, where it emerges for the

---

1   These underground *karéz* are found in the Turfan oasis of Chinese Turkistan, all through Baluchistan, and in many parts of Persia. In Persia they are more usually called *qanat* – E.O.L.

first time into the open. The water is kept thus under cover to prevent its evaporating in the great heat on its way down into the valley.

By way of Imam Quli and Chinaran – both of them surrounded by fortification walls – I reached Meshed, the Holy City of the Shiahs. My first visit was to Qannadi's uncle, who lived here and acted in eastern Persia as buyer for his nephew. From him I borrowed a hundred tumans. The worthy Husain Zada almost had an apoplectic fit when he recognised me. Laughing, I gave him an outline of my adventures, and heard that Qannadi had long ago given me up and had sent my savings to my relatives in Vienna. I begged Husain Zada not to breathe a word to Qannadi of my reappearance, for I wanted the pleasure of surprising him in person in Tabriz.

The sole European shop in Meshed belonged to an Englishman called Tink. Here I bought myself a decent suit, along with some shirts and collars. Then I betook myself to the *hammam* or Turkish bath and submitted to a thorough cleansing. I cannot deny that for the first few days I felt thoroughly uncomfortable in my new clothes. The collar of my shirt was the worst. I had got so unused to a collar that I had to keep taking it off, and only by slow degrees did I reaccustom myself to this badge of civilisation.

The baths in Persian provincial towns, in contrast to those in Turkistan, are usually above and not below the ground. The bather is not permitted to wash himself as with us. Whether you like it or not, you must put yourself in the hands of the servants, who simply take possession of you and get on with their job.

After being stripped I had several buckets of ice-cold water thrown over me, which were immediately followed by several buckets of hot, then cold again, and so on. When I fled into a corner of the room, breathless and swearing at the prospect of another threatened cold douche, I was seized and forcibly dragged into the centre of the bathroom while half a dozen eggs were broken over my head, so that their contents flowed all down my body. Three pairs of hands now began to massage me with the yolk and white

199

and that with such vigour that after this procedure I fell to the ground and just lay there, half-dead with exhaustion. A few more ice-cold douches brought me hastily to my feet again. If I had not been at the moment too weak and tired I should certainly have hammered the conscientious bathmen, who were after all only doing their duty by me and would have been justifiably offended. As it was, I meekly submitted and endured what was to follow. They rolled me over on my stomach and began to rub down my back with balls of camels' hair, then turned me over and treated the other side in the same way till I looked like a boiled lobster. Next, every joint was kneaded and tugged till it cracked as if it were being dislocated, then my whole body was beaten and pummelled with the back of their hands by my tormentors, as if I were a tough beefsteak. Finally I was indulged with another cold douche. Then, like a living corpse, I was carried into an ante-room and regaled with tea. There are no story-tellers in the Persian baths such as are provided in Turkistan, obviously because after their violent man-handling the guests are in no condition to listen to them. I slept soundly for two hours and woke feeling as if I had been reborn.

Qannadi's uncle had insisted on my taking up my quarters in his house, which was much to my advantage, for he would accept no payment. I wanted to spend a few days in Meshed to recover from the hardships of my travels, and then proceed by forced marches to Tabriz and thence – HOME. I made no further attempt to keep homesickness at bay, and in imagination I often saw myself quietly seated in a Vienna café, reading a paper and drinking Mocha.

During the day I strolled about Meshed and visited the tombs of Ali, Imam Riza, and Harun ar Rashid, but they are strictly closed to Unbelievers. In Turkistan the Faithful are unperturbed if they see a European in their mosques. I saw once more the magnificent mosque of Gohar Shad, with its cupola of water-blue tiles and its golden minarets; and the most lovely building in all Persia, the shrine built beyond the north-west gate by Shah Abbas, which, with the Sanctuary of the Sacred Quarter, is the pride of Meshed. The Sacred Quarter is enclosed all round by chains and strictly

Muharram. The litter with the 'Corpse' of Ali being carried across the square

reserved for mullas and muftis. It may be entered by pilgrims and the ordinary Muslim inhabitants only on certain days of festival. It is possible to continue down the main street of the bazaar, which runs through the sanctuary, only by making a long detour round the sacred enclosure. Carriages must likewise drive round, for the chains may in no circumstances be violated.

Husain Zada conveyed to me one day that I had better be getting on, for the ceremonies of the Muharram would be starting in a few days, and most of the Europeans settled in Meshed took care to be absent for at least the first ten days of it, to avoid any possibilities of friction, which were as unwelcome to the Persian authorities as to the foreign consulates. Only a year ago (July 1924) the American consul, Major Robert Imbrie, had been stoned in the open street and literally torn to pieces when the fanatical Shiahs observed him taking photographs of the Muharram procession. The celebrations themselves had nothing new to offer me, for I had watched them at close quarters in exceptionally favourable circumstances in Meshed in 1916; I had now thoroughly recovered, and homesickness was growing acute, so I willingly fell in with his suggestion.

But Fate saw otherwise. I had made all my preparations for the start and booked a seat in the motor-bus which had been running since the preceding spring between Meshed and Tehran. The very day before the weekly bus was due to leave I went down with a severe attack of fever and could not think of travelling. It was six days before I was well enough to get up, but by that time Muharram had begun and a start was for the moment out of the question, so willy-nilly I had to stay where I was, till the tenth day of the solemnities should be safely over.

Muharram is the ceremonial mourning for the deaths of Husain and, in a lesser degree, of Hasan, the grandsons of the Prophet Muhammad, and wherever Shiahs are found the anniversary is most solemnly celebrated. The tenth day is the most eventful and impressive of the whole ceremonial. I have described these mourning scenes in full detail in my earlier book, *Pascholl, Plenny!* already

202

alluded to. What I saw on this occasion was an exact repetition of
the scenes of 1916.

Meshed. Muharram. Some of the seriously wounded are carried off. In the
foreground men can be seen with blood flowing over their clothes

After the usual circular procession and the mimic battle, which
passed off somewhat more quietly this year, some two hundred
men with closely shaven heads appeared in the open square,
wearing white trousers and long white shirts, and each holding a
short, well-sharpened sabre in his hand. When they arrived the
whole immense multitude went mad and began shouting 'Husain!'
without intermission. The men took up their positions in pairs
facing each other and stamped the ground with their bare feet in
time to an intoxicating music, till they were soon smothered in a
cloud of dust. Presently they began to smite each other with their
sabres, inflicting wounds on head and arms till their white clothes
were soaked with blood. With grotesque leaps they bounded round
the square shouting: 'O Husain! O Hasan!' Each could look into
the other's face and see the wounds he had inflicted, the sight of

the other's blood inflamed his passion, and presently the shouting faded into guttural groaning. Puddles of gore formed on the ground, and the sweet, sickly smell of blood combined with the intense heat made me feel so ill that I was actually sick. Fortunately I was so well concealed on the roof of a serai belonging to an Englishman that I could not be seen by the fanatical mob.

Numbers of bleeding men had fallen unconscious to the ground, and the rest of the leaping fanatics struck at them with their sabres till at last some police forced their way through the howling crowd, lifted up the victims, and carried them away. Another troop of police, greatly daring, attempted to persuade some of the more seriously wounded who seemed about to faint to allow themselves to be removed before they were completely cut to bits.

This religious fanaticism is highly repugnant to us, but to the Shiahs it is a supreme act of holiness which arouses their highest admiration. The men who thus cut themselves to pieces have attained the certainty – whatever sins they may have committed in this life – of being received direct into Paradise when they die. Even the spectators are absolved from all transgressions against the Quran.

When the butchering episode was over, a new troop of men approached, bare to the waist. These began also to cry: 'Husain!' and with their clenched fists beat their breasts till they resounded. Their chests were soon bruised and swollen and red with unshed blood; then they started an incoherent dance, thrusting their heads forward with a sudden jerk till foam issued from their lips, and one after another fell to the ground and rolled in the blood-soaked dust left by his predecessors. After this, a large covered litter, representing the tomb of Ali, was carried across the square and the day's ceremony was over. Not for me, however. For days I could not rid myself of the smell of blood or the vision of those gaping wounds – though my nerves, thank God, are pretty tough.

XV

The Caravan Roads of North Persia

There was nothing further to prevent my setting out. The rattling tin kettle – a production of General Motors, Ltd. – carried me via Nishapur, Sabzawar, Mihr , Mazinan – where one famous day the march through of the British troops had badly put the wind up me – Abbasabad, Miandasht, and Maiamai to the town of Shahrud, where I had to wait for a further bus connection.

The Persian towns and villages which we passed through were as uniform and monotonous as the serais of the places where we put up for the night. We would halt at midday, either by a tea-house or somewhere in the desert or amongst the hills, and make a fire close beside the road to prepare a primitive meal. I felt happy and light-hearted when a breeze from the north, blowing down off the Jaghatai mountains, brought a breath of refreshment. These mountains run parallel to and on the right of the road the whole 375 miles from Nishapur to Shahrud. When the wind, on the other hand, blew from the south across the great *kavir*, or salt desert, forever carrying sand and salt-dust in its train, I cursed like a trooper and wished the drive well over. When we came to a serai at night I first washed off from my body the thick crust of sweat and sand, drank a few bowls of tea, and sank at once, dead weary, into a heavy sleep, from which even the biting of the lice and the crawling of spiders and scorpions were unavailing to wake me before morning.

From Shahrud the new bus took us via Deh i Mulla, Damghan, Daulatabad, and Gusha to Simnan, where my fellow travellers and I were held up for three days in consequence of a breakdown that occurred just before we reached Simnan. A broken axle had to be removed and a new one fetched from Tehran. Simnan is one of the most important caravan junctions of Persia, for it is the terminus of the one and only route across the western *kavir*.

I was within an ace of embarking on a new journey from here. The Devil, who is lord of all dangers and adventures, waged a long and bitter battle with my longing for home – and nearly won the victory.

'Look here,' he cried, 'in all your life you will never have another chance of seeing the *kavir*! Seize it while you may! After all what does it matter – a few weeks more or less?'

'No,' said Home. 'You must not venture into the salt desert. For years you have been possessed by the devil of adventure, and have yielded to his wiles and travelled quite enough over mountains and across deserts. It is time to return.'

'Stuff and nonsense!' retorted the Devil. 'How many Europeans have ever crossed the salt desert? Shouldn't you love to be one of the few?'

'Don't listen to him!' whispered Home. 'Thousands have perished in the *kavir*. Do you want to be one of the many? Think of the mountains and forests of Austria! Aren't they preferable to these sun-cursed wastes of salt?'

As it happened I was at the moment almost dead of thirst, and would gladly have given every penny I possessed for a drink of cool spring water, so the Devil lost the battle, and as the motor-bus spluttered up the steep road to Firuzkuh on its way to Tehran, I contented myself with a glance over the northern margin of the *kavir* and the immense salt basin that stretched away out of sight below. Just after this the bus drove into a gorge and the desert vanished from my sight. Farewell, *kavir*! It was not to be. What good would it have been, anyway!

After we left the gorge the road afforded a view northwards to an ancient holy place, the grave of some saint, built like a small fortress on the mountain side. Then the highest mountain in Persia came in sight, the eternal ice and snow-fields of Demavend. It lifts its blunt crater cone nearly 18,000 feet into the sky, into which it seems insensibly to blend. Immediately afterwards we passed through the town of Demavend, and all the way to Tehran the great mountain kept peeping at us through valleys and ravines, till in the later afternoon it donned a cap of cloud and withdrew itself from human gaze.

O Tehran! How you have changed since I last saw you! Immense revolutions have taken place in Persia. On the 12th of December 1924 the Grand Wazir and Dictator, in defiance of Parliament, drove the last of the Qajars from the throne and so ended a dynasty which had ruled Persia for a hundred and thirty-one years. He wrested from Parliament the hereditary kingship and the title of Shah Riza Pahlavi, and since then styles himself, after the fashion alike of the great Darius and of his inglorious recent successors: Shahan Shah, or King of Kings. When I reached Tehran it was a bare nine months since the accession of the new Shah, and some four years since his march on Tehran, but the force of his personality, his indomitable will, and his inexhaustible energy – a characteristic incomprehensible to the Persians – had worked genuine miracles even in this short space of time. With relentless severity he opened campaigns against banditry, the filth of the towns, the corruption of officials, and the general passion for slavish imitation of the foreigner.

The safety of the great caravan routes is as much the work of the new Shah as the installation of motor-buses. The robber bands of Shah-Sewand and Kurd were threatened with annihilation; corrupt officials – and their number was legion – were prosecuted, masses of them were dismissed from office and executed: a proceeding which won the Shah the unqualified approval of his people, who had at first eyed askance his rise to power.

In the last ten years Shah Riza Pahlavi has raised the strength of his defensive forces to a pitch which would make an attack on the country a catastrophe for the aggressor, where in olden days it would have been an uneventful picnic. An admirably disciplined army, a railway from the Caspian to the Persian Gulf nearly completed, and an excellent network of roads throughout the country have prepared Persia for any contingency, and now in 1936 she has no mind to let herself be passively partitioned between Russia and England.

The age-long rivalry between these powers, quickened anew by the battle for the oil wells of Persia, would sooner or later have been bound to lead to the dismemberment of the country.

This danger was imminent during the World War. But in the hour of her greatest need an unexpected factor came into play which ultimately set Persia's feet on the road to freedom. German, Austrian, and Hungarian soldiers, escaping from the Russian prison camps of Turkistan, rallied in Tehran to the number of three hundred, and under the leadership of the German Military Attaché, Count Kanitz, and of Consul Schünemann formed a nucleus of picked men which was quickly joined by all the Germans, Austrians, Hungarians, and Turks in Persia at that time. Several Swedish officers with their Persian gendarmes came to swell the little force. When it had shown its mettle by various victories over British and Russians in Persia, Persian adventurers and patriots flocked to its colours. It reached its zenith in numbers and success after Count Kanitz had proclaimed a Holy War. The miniature army suffered sorely both by casualties and disease, and the incompetence of the Persian Government ultimately compelled it to withdraw into Turkey by way of Baghdad. Nevertheless its exploits had destroyed the myth of British and Russian omnipotence. Bands of volunteers and free lances carried on guerrilla campaigns in all directions and inflicted severe losses on the armies of occupation, till the two governments decided to give up their plans for dividing Persia between them.

After the end of the War the diplomatic battles for Persia began. It was highly inconvenient for the Soviets to be obliged to set aside large forces to garrison a perpetually rebellious territory, the more especially as they were sufficiently occupied putting down rising after rising in Turkistan, and were therefore, as it were, continuously between two fires. They thereupon decided on a magnanimous gesture, withdrew their garrisons, and made the Persians a

Tehran. Qajar Mosque with golden dome. The second most sacred shrine
in Persia, the shrine of Fatima, sister of Iman Rizah

gift of the roads they had constructed, and the fifty-three or fifty-four miles of railway from Julfa to Tabriz.

Riza Shah maintained friendly relations with Soviet Russia, and Persia was one of the first countries to recognise the Union of Socialist Soviet Republics. The Russians did not neglect to use their opportunity to make their influence felt. There was at one point great danger of the Bolshevization of Persia. But in the bloody campaigns of many years against recalcitrant provinces the new Shah demonstrated that his object was not Communism but the unity of Persia. When his last opponent, Kuchak Khan, fled to meet a tragic end in the forests, Riza Shah was left the unquestioned and independent monarch of all Persia.

In the bazaar in Tehran I lighted on Russman, Kuchak Khan's ex-adjutant, officiating – as a tailor. Russman started as a sergeant-major of Dragoons in the Austrian Army and was taken prisoner by the Russians. He was confined in the prison camp at Ashqabad and succeeded in escaping to Bukhara, where he attained the rank of a general of cavalry. The story goes that at the end of each week – the Muslim Friday corresponds of course to the Christian Sunday – Russman always got so drunk that the Amir took his rank and titles from him every Friday, but he was obliged to reinstate him every Monday morning, for there was no one else who could command his divisions. Russman knew no Persian, which is the language of the Bukharan Army, and had consequently introduced German when training his cavalry regiments, which consisted entirely of new recruits. Incidentally he had thus rendered himself indispensable, since there was no one else in the place who knew German. From Bukhara he found his way to Persia, offered his services to Kuchak Khan, and was sent to Baku as his plenipotentiary. The Soviets placed at his disposal a ship loaded with guns, rifles, and ammunition. Russman sailed with it to Enzeli and handed it over to Kuchak Khan, who was thus enabled to take up the struggle against Riza Pahlavi. When Kuchak Khan's army was defeated Russman felt he had had enough of adventuring and bethought himself that he had once upon a time learnt the tailoring trade in Linz. He set up in Tehran and has been busy ever since stitching European clothes for the inhabitants of the Persian capital.

I had been hearing endless legends about him for years, but it was quite by chance that I learned of his presence in Tehran. When I addressed him in German the sometime cavalry general and Communist commandant of a man-of-war, now the Tehran tailor, responded with a somewhat wistful smile. He was sitting on his hunkers on the floor of his workshop, exactly like a native, and vigorously turning the handle of his sewing machine. 'Well, how goes it, Herr Russman? Aren't you longing to get home to Austria again?'

No, he wasn't. He had almost forgotten his mother tongue. His whole appearance and manner betrayed that he had come to feel himself more of an Oriental than a European. Ten years of adventure amongst Bukharans and Persians had metamorphosed him completely. He had long ago embraced Islam and taken an Afghan wife. I had the greatest difficulty in persuading him to tell me something of his variegated career. But once he got started the flood-gates of his eloquence suddenly burst, and I could scarcely contain myself for astonishment – though I have lived through a thing or two myself. Russman's reminiscences would fill a library. I must confess that I believed only about 10 per cent of what he told me, till various Persian officers with whom I discussed him showed me my error. There is probably no European who has got to know Bukhara and Persia so thoroughly as the modest little tailor at No. 71 Muremda Khan, Tehran.

The new Shah, who was fifty-eight at the time of my stay in Tehran, had already built himself an aerodrome and set about revolutionising the architecture of his capital.

After being overwhelmed by the impression of the monumental Shimran Gate with its frescoes and tilework, and the Qaswin Gate with its brilliant mosaics and its four little towers, and by the Qajar Mosque, the sightseer is strung up to the highest pitch of expectation when he comes to visit the Shams ul Amara, the world-famous Palace of the Persian Kings. This lofty building, some five stories high, towers above the roofs of the city, its entrance gate flanked by double towers clothed with blue-green tiles. It seems to promise all the wonders of the Orient. But disappointment awaits you. Your first hope is to get a sight of the loveliest of lovely things, the famous Peacock Throne and the immense Marble Throne. The Peacock Throne of Delhi, composed of pure gold and precious stones, was brought from India by Nadir Shah: its jewels have long since been replaced by glass imitations! The later Qajars sold some of the jewels in Moscow and Paris, and used the rest to cover loans in London. Even the tiniest sliver of diamond in the most hidden cavity is common window glass. The precious stones, literally beyond all price, have been scattered to the four winds of heaven, and nothing genuine is left but the gold itself. The Marble Throne has fared little better. The great monster stands over twelve feet high in an open loggia. If you want to see it at close quarters you have to go round a large basin, paddle across a spring, and climb some steps up past twisted columns. The throne itself stands on a sort of platform borne aloft by marble figures, in a large niche adorned with mirrors the glass of which has all gone black. The mirror ceiling of the great hall itself has suffered almost equally. One might reasonably expect to find in Tehran, 'The Centre of the Universe', as the Qajars used to call it, such genuine oriental art as rejoices the heart at every step in Isfahan, for instance. The remaining rooms of the great palace are equally disappointing, but it is understood that they are all soon to be overhauled by the express order of the Shah.

The Picture Gallery, which contains portraits of a large number of European rulers, including the Tsar Nicholas II, the Emperor Franz-Josef I, the Kaiser William II, etc., shows about as much sense of style as a jumble sale. The staircase leading to the State Rooms suggests an old curiosity shop such as abound in the Tandelmarkt in Vienna. Gilded plaster statues, glass balls in red and silver, like those that disfigure the public gardens in small provincial towns, ornament the wide balustrades, while here and there between these monstrosities there stands a really valuable Chinese or ancient

Japanese vase. Behind a large oil-lamp with an impossibly hideous shade there is a magnificent casket of loveliest alabaster, on which some barbarian has scribbled his name in ink. These various 'treasures' were collected by the shahs Muzaffar ud Din, Muhammad Ali, Ahmad, the last of the Qajars, and his heir the Waliahd, and here they have been indiscriminately dumped together in complete confusion. A bathroom dedicated to the use of the royal heir was papered from top to bottom with worthless oleographs of female nudities. Riza Shah has already thrown out a lot of rubbish and before long the whole palace will no doubt be cleared of its trumpery. The only thing which is to be retained in its original form is the hall with the Peacock Throne, on which the new Shah took his seat that the crown of ancient Persia might be placed upon his head.

With a sigh of immense relief the visitor quits the tawdry interior and steps into the glorious gardens of the palace. The guides murmur with awe as they confide that all the 'artistic treasures' have been removed. The whole park used to be desecrated by stags in sheet iron, abominable grottos, and every imaginable horror of the kind. The immemorial trees and the basins of water, skilfully connected with each other by ingenious channels, need in truth no other ornament than the gay flower-beds and the many spring-fed streams which skirt the narrow paths.

One of the well-known sights of Tehran is the Maidan i Sipah, the Square of the Guns. Along one side of the high stone walls that enclose the palace and the ministries there stood until a few months ago a long row of cannon, which served a triple purpose. First they formed a collection of every kind of firing implement from every epoch of Persia's rise and fall; secondly they were a symbol of the rulers' might and silently proclaimed to malcontents: 'Behold, the strength of Persia's Kings!' and thirdly, until the coming of Riza Shah, they were used as the means of public executions. Until 1921 the cannon would thunder across the square and every shot cost some Persian his life. Riza Shah had these symbols of terror taken away, and ordered the whole blood-soaked ground to be dug over, so that no Persian need tread on his brethren's blood. Where once the executioner's cannon stood there is now a large pillar on which are posted up the announcements of cinemas and places of entertainment. A few paces off a white-gloved policeman stands on a raised plinth under an umbrella and regulates the considerable traffic. The rest of the Maidan i Sipah has been converted into a park with a conservatory, and outside the iron railing of the park is the terminus of the many lines of motor-buses which connect Tehran with every corner of the kingdom. A wall two stories high sheltering an enormous number of bazaar booths forms a worthy background to the square.

Clouds of dust are rising, beams are crashing, old walls are toppling – the ancient *chai-khanas* and coffee-houses round the square are being pulled down to make room for broad streets down which a few months hence electric trams will be running. Up till now the 300,000 inhabitants of the Persian capital have been served by leisurely horse-trams, which dawdle through the streets with clanging bells. 'Haste is of the devil,' says a Persian proverb! High poles are springing up everywhere, which are to carry telephone, telegraph, and electric light to the remotest corners of the city. Hitherto only the very centre of the city boasted electric light; a few paces behind the Maidan i Sipah oil-lamps burnt dimly in dirty lanterns. Uncovered water-channels – distributing disease as liberally as water – have coursed through the town, as through every other oriental town, since the memory of man, and are dreaded by Europeans as much as they are loved by the native population. They likewise are doomed to disappearance in favour of a modern water-supply. We of western Europe, who take underground sewers, pipe water, gas, electricity, and water-closets for granted, can only dimly conceive the courage needed to impose such installations on a backward people. Hand in hand with the Shah's campaigns against Persian indolence and indifference marches the development of an organised school system. A new law makes school attendance obligatory in every town of over 20,000 inhabitants, most of which have hitherto possessed no educational establishment of any kind. Intermediate schools and universities where the exact sciences are taught are crowding out the religious madrasahs, which in future may be attended only by students desirous of entering the priesthood. The people must learn reading, writing, and Persian history in recognised schools, for the new Shah is determined to restore Persia to its earlier fame as a land of culture, in defiance of the saying current this hundred years: 'Persia is an ancient land of culture. It has lost its culture and kept nothing but its age.'

I had had a thorough rest and was feeling fit again. In the Maidan i Sipah I boarded a motor-bus bound for Tabriz. When we got to Qazwin our driver was ordered by the police to abandon the good route by Sultania and Kekben in favour of the much worse road by Manjil and Qabakh, for large bands of rebels were reported to be active between Kekben and Mianah. We left Qaswin followed by a motor-lorry carrying twenty soldiers and a mounted machine-gun. The soldiers had instructions to see us safely to Mianah. Along wretched roads and over half-crumbled bridges we drove through the valley of the Qizil Uzen. On steep bits of the road we often had to get down and help to push our bus over the obstacles. Wherever we halted the soldiers swarmed out of their lorry. They rightly felt that the great boulders that had held us up might well prove to be an ambush. Nothing untoward happened, however, not a shot was fired, and not a single Shah-Sewand obliged the soldiers by presenting a target for their machine-gun. It was the last rainy season which had brought down large rocks and masses of debris from the mountain sides and flung them across the road, but the officer in command of our escort preferred to see in the business the hand of rebels rather than the hand of nature.

We reached Qabakh unmolested. From this on we were accompanied by a second motor-bus carrying soldiers and a searchlight, whose dazzling beams explored the road and the rock walls alongside for hundreds of yards in front of us. Riza Shah was certainly doing his utmost to ensure the safety of travellers on the

Persian roads. It was almost midnight before we drove through the Ardabil Gate into Mianah.

It seemed doubtful next morning whether the motor-bus would proceed to Tabriz or not, for the road ahead lay in the main sphere of the restless and rebel Shah-Sewand. They are the last real nomads left in western Persia and hitherto they have succeeded in maintaining their independence. The tribe can put in the field 70,000 armed and well-mounted men, and in their impregnable mountain fastnesses of Azerbaijan they have successfully defied every attempt to subdue them. Under the preceding rulers such attempts as were made to render them innocuous were very half-hearted, for they maintained an undying feud with the equally rebellious Kurds, and thus saved the Government the trouble of keeping the Kurds at bay. They also formed a valuable buffer against both Russia and Turkey. Both these states had interests of their own in the frontier regions between Lake Urmia and the Caspian, and each sought to enlist the help of the Shah-Sewand against the other and against the Persian Government. This game of political intrigue delighted the Shah-Sewand. They accepted gold and weapons impartially from Turk and Russian and then acted as best suited themselves without regard to the plans or wishes of their patrons. In recent years, however, when Riza Shah found that the Shah-Sewand completely disregarded their promises to keep the roads safe for travellers, he sent some of his best troops against them and was successful in executing the leaders and disarming several of the clans.

It grew towards evening and the postmaster could still say nothing definite about the prospects of our starting. There were rumours of heavy fighting in progress round Haji Agha, while the alternative, more roundabout route by the shores of Lake Urmia to Tabriz was reported to be in the hands of the Shah-Sewand, who were engaged in battle with a large body of Kurdish levies. The Kurds had responded only too gladly to the invitations of the Shah so as to pursue the feud against their hereditary foes under the guise of legitimate warfare. The net result was that the whole region to the west of Mianah was one great battlefield. Troops and detachments of gendarmerie were marching through the town or taking up their quarters there. The whole little place was soon overcrowded with military and the price of provisions had soared within a few days to ten times the normal. There are few towns in Persia with which I have not a direct personal acquaintance, and, though the average of attractiveness is not high, I know of none to compare with Mianah in dismal misery, so I was impatient to shake the dust of it from my feet. Our hopes of an early start seemed to grow more and more uncertain, and I was seriously thinking of buying myself a horse and continuing my journey in company with one or the other of the military forces passing through. On the fifth day, however, we were told that the motor-buses were going to set out with a detachment of military lorries.

About thirty lorries with soldiers and some light artillery drove ahead of us, then followed four civilian motor-buses and some dozen more military lorries, while a Persian Cossack regiment brought up the rear. In the rare moments when the appalling cloud of dust raised by motors and horsemen opened for a second I caught glimpses of the distant snowfields of the Sahend Mountains, the guardians of Tabriz. There must have been severe fighting at Haji Agha, for we saw exhausted horses, the corpses of Shah-Sewand and Persian soldiers, weapons and equipment of every kind, lying strewn along the road, and the place itself had been bombarded and burned down. There had been no time to tidy up, for the military were pursuing the flying Shah-Sewand towards Sarab, hoping to drive them into the arms of the Cossacks advancing from Ardabil. The villages in East Persia are all provided with strong and lofty fortress towers as a defence against the raiding Turkomans, and here we found the villages similarly fortified against Kurds and Shah-Sewand. All these village strongholds were now garrisoned with armed soldiers to guard against surprise attacks. Cannon and machine-guns had been mounted on all the surrounding heights, showing that in spite of their recent victory the troops felt none too secure in a country where every ravine might at any moment disgorge a strong body of rebels. Soldiers of every arm were encamped in Turkman Chai, on their way back after a battle on the Aji Chai. They had many Shah-Sewand prisoners with them, whom they fettered hand and foot and flung about like bales of goods. An officer noticed me as the sole European amongst the travellers and addressed me in German. I ventured to call his attention to this inhuman treatment of the prisoners. He only shrugged his shoulders and told me that not a single Persian soldier had survived who had had the misfortune to be taken by the Shah-Sewand; they had been tortured to death. In corroboration of his statement he bade me look at some of the soldiers' bodies which the rebels had left behind. I saw masses of almost unrecognisable human flesh, gruesomely mutilated. Death must have come to these wretches as a release.

As we proceeded we heard heavy rifle fire and isolated cannon shots near Shibli. Presently a dip in the valley gave us a view of a pass ahead in which fighting was going on. While the Persian soldiers in their dark uniforms were clearly distinguishable among the grey rocks, the enemy remained invisible. Only the frequent little puffs of smoke which appeared and vanished on the crest of the pass gave a clue to their position. An invisible Persian battery kept up continuous fire without inflicting any perceptible damage on the enemy, whose fire seemed to increase rather than diminish. We had halted a little while to watch this unusual spectacle of fighting actually in progress. The Shah-Sewand apparently spotted us, for I heard the all too familiar 'whizz-whizz' of bullets unpleasantly close, and splinters of stone sprang into the air as one struck the ground near our bus. Our driver accelerated and fled at top speed beyond range.

We passed through various Kurdish villages, whose inhabitants were coolly going about their daily work, and ultimately reached Tabriz.

In Tabriz all was quiet. The Shah-Sewand had not dared to attack the strong garrison and nothing save the presence of the wounded gave a hint of the battles which had been taking place so near the town. In Tabriz I was at home. The lanes and squares, the mosques and tea-houses were old and well-loved friends. Through numerous orchards I made my way on foot to Lilava, the European quarter, in which Abul Qasim Qannadi, hundred-per-cent Persian though he is, has his house, his ware-rooms, and his office. I had bidden him good-bye for a month that day in Barfurush; the Prodigal was returning at last, sixteen months later. It was afternoon as I came to Qannadi's, climbed the steep wooden stair, and peeped cautiously in through the open door. My worthy chief was sitting at his writing-table, painting figures into his account book.

As my shadow darkened the door he looked up. 'Salam aleikum, Brother Qannadi!' I cried.

A loud crash followed. Qannadi had fallen off his chair in sheer amazement.

Notes

The 'Rishta' or Guinea-Worm (p. 15)

Krist's assumption that this unpleasant and dangerous parasite is found only in the stagnant waters of Bukhara is baseless.

As its English name 'Guinea-worm', and its Latin names *Filaria* (or *Dracununculus*) *medinensis* imply, it is all too well known in West Africa and Arabia. His estimate of maximum length as nine feet is also unduly pessimistic, though doubtless to a sufferer from whom the worm is being extracted by tiny fractions of an inch, it may well appear miles long.

I summarize an article on the subject from A. G. Chandler's *Introduction to Human Parasitology*, New York and London, Fifth Edition, 1936:

The guinea-worm is one of the scourges of life in western Asia from central India to Arabia, as well as in Egypt, much of central Africa, and some localities of tropical America.

The 'fiery serpents' which molested the Israelites by the Red Sea were not improbably guinea-worms.

The adult female worm lives in the deeper layers of subcutaneous tissue till it breaks the skin of its host to give birth to myriads of wriggling young. It reaches a length of from two and a half to four feet, with a diameter of one to one and a half millimetres, thus resembling a long piece of cord or coarse thread (Persian: *rishta*). The males are scarcely known, but would appear to be mere midgets of one to one and a half inches.

When ready to bring forth its young, the female is instinctively

221

attracted to the surface skin of its host, especially to such parts as frequently come into contact with cold water: the arms of women who wash clothes on a river bank, the legs and back of a water-carrier.

The infant worm at birth is about 0.60 to 0.75 millimetres long. It can survive in the water only for a few days, unless it can find harbourage in a cyclops. Twelve days to two months inside this minute crustacean fit it for its next adventure. It is by then about one millimetre in length.

Human beings become the unwilling hosts of the guinea-worm by drinking water from wells and ponds containing the minute cyclops which is harboring the guinea-worm. In some places up to twenty-five per cent of the population are incapacitated for a month each year by the septic ulcer caused. This first appears as a blister, the poison of which may bring on urticaria, nausea, vomiting, diarrhoea, giddiness, or fainting.

The primitive method of extraction practised by Krist – though modified by anti-sepsis and longer incisions – is still the essence of up-to-date treatment, drugs and ointments having proved almost valueless. If the worm breaks in the process of extraction blood-poisoning, involving amputation or even death, may ensue.

If water is even roughly filtered through muslin this is sufficient to remove the cyclops and therewith the guinea-worm larva. It is a curious fact that if methods of drawing water are adopted which do not involve the immersion of the drawer's body, guinea-worm disappears. Government education and intervention have completely eliminated the plague from many places in India.

The 'Chervonitz' (p. 34)

I owe the following note on Soviet Russian currency to the courtesy of Messrs. Thos. Cook & Son (Bankers), Ltd., London, W.1:

'In 1924 all the old currency having been demonetized, a new currency was issued by the Soviet Government on a gold basis. The unit was the chervonitz of ten roubles, and the gold parity against sterling being £1 1s. 1¾d. per gold chervonitz.

'By 1926 this new currency had already depreciated by about 10 per cent, but with practically no dealings in the currency outside Russia the internal value was artificially maintained.'

Calculating on these data Krist's 31 roubles would in 1926 have represented approximately £2 18s. 6¼d. of English money.

E.O.L.

List of Vernacular Words

Whatever may have been the original languages of Central Asia in prehistoric times, the country has, throughout history, been swept by successive waves of invasion and conquest – Mongol, Arab, Persian, and more recently Russian. Probably the majority of the inhabitants of Central Asia today speak some dialect of Turki, itself a variety of Turkish proper, but various dialects of Persian, such as Tajiki, are also widely current, and the Turki vocabulary is full of Persian elements as Persian is of Arabic.

A large number of Central Asian place-names are significant: Tash Qurghan = Rock Fortress is pure Turki; Surkh Ab = Red Water (river) is pure Persian; while Char Su is a hybrid – Persian *Char* = Four, plus Turki *Su* = Water (river).

Many names whose meaning is less immediately obvious may be of Mongol origin. I know of no comprehensive study of the Mongol language elements surviving in Central Asia whether in the ordinary vocabulary or in place-names; but the following tentative list of vernacular words will enable the curious reader to interpret such names occuring in the present book as are composed of Arabic, Turkish (Turki), or Persian elements.

A., Arabic

T., Turkish or Turki

P., Persian

R., Russian

PA., Persian, borrowed or derived from Arabic, and so forth

E.O.L.

LIST OF VERNACULAR WORDS

ab (P.), water

abad (P.), city, habitation, cultivated land. Used as suffix forming names of towns and villages

afshan (P.), verbal root signifying 'scattering'. *Zerafshan*, gold-scattering

aji (T.), bitter

al (A.), the definite article 'the'. In compounds frequently assimilated to a following consonant: *ar-*, *ash-*, *ad-*, etc. In certain cases appears as *ul* or *il*, the vowel representing the case-ending of the preceding word

ala (T.), piebald, multi-coloured

amir (A.), king, 'Amir', pl. *umara*

airan (T.), thick, sour milk (camel's, goat's, mare's)

aq (T.), white

aq-saqal (T.), white-beard, elder, headman

arabah (PA.), high-wheeled cart; v. page 143

archa (T.), juniper

archa-chik (T.), guardian of the juniper forests

arghali (P.), species of wild, mountain sheep

ariq (T.), irrigation channel, water-course, canal

arwat (A.), pl. of *rabat*, q.v., rest-house, inn

aul (T.), semi-permanent nomad encampment, village

baigha (T.), wild game played on horseback in which the 'ball' is the carcass of a sheep; v. pp. 27, 124

bala (P.), upper, raised, above

bala-khana (P.), balcony, upper room

baqsi (T.), medicine-man

bashi (T.), leader, person in command, head, 'boss'

batir (T.), cattle-thief. Possibly a corruption of P. *bahadur*, hero, champion

bazar (P.), shopping-centre, street (frequently roofed-in) of open, booth-like shops, 'bazaar'

bazar-jik (P. + T.), pedlar, hawker

beg (T.), Turkish official, governor

bulak (T.), spring (of water)

bumaga (R.), passport, permit, identification papers

buran (T.), sandstorm

buzah (T.), intoxicating drink, made by Qirghiz from mares' milk

1. *chai* (T.), river
2. *chai* (P.), tea. Drunk in Central Asia with salt and fat.

Chai i shirin, sweetened tea, drunk with sugar

chai-khana (P.), tea-house, tea-shop, inn

chai-khana-ji, chai-khana-chik (P. + T.), keeper of tea-house

char (P.), four

chilim (P.), hubble-bubble pipe. The tobacco-smoke is drawn through cold water before being inhaled. (Probably derived from Hindi)

charas, chars (P.), preparation of Indian hemp. Used as narcotic

-chik, -jik, -ji (T.), person in charge of, or professionally connected with, something

chimat (T.), woman's horse-hair veil

chol (T.), desert

chuchka (T.), pig

dab (T.), customary law amongst Qirghiz. A corruption of PA., *adab*

dagh, tagh (T.), mountain range, mountain

dasht (P.), desert

dil (P.), heart

din (P.), faith, religion. Especially 'The Faith', i.e. Islam

deh (P.), village

feringi (P.), 'Frank', any European. A word common throughout the Near and Middle East and probably dating from the time of the Crusades

garm (P.), warm, hot

gök, kok (T.), blue, green. A large number of eastern languages use the same word to denote 'blue' and 'green', adding, if necessary, some qualifying word to distinguish the two colours

gul (P.), flower

gulchem (T.), edible, garlic-like root. Found in the Trans-Alai and used by the Qirghiz as a bread-substitute

guzar (P.), ford, crossing-place

haji (PA.), one who has performed the Pilgrimage to Mecca

hauz (PA.), reservoir, tank, artificial pond, or basin of water

hazrat (A.), noble, holy; title of respect. Prefixed to proper names of saints, etc., and hence used in names of places named after them

i (P.), 1. denoting genitive case: Deh i Mulla, *the mulla's village*

2. linking noun and adjective: Deh i Nau, also Deinau, *the new village.*

insha' Allah (A.), God willing, please God, 'Good-bye'. A phrase in constant use throughout all Muslim countries

Islam (A.). The religion of 'submission' (to the will of God) taught by the Prophet Muhammad. Its votaries object to being called 'Muhammadans', since they do not worship their prophet nor claim divine honours for him

-istan (P.), place of . . ., country of . . . Rigistan, place of sand, open square; Tajikistan, the country of the Tajiks, etc.

-jand (T.), v. *-qand*

-ji, -jik (T.), v. *-chik*

kafir (A.), Unbeliever, i.e. non-Muslim

kand (P.), town, village

kavir (P.), salt-ground, salt desert

khan (TP.), chief, lord

khana (P.), house, dwelling

khilat (AP.), man's robe or cloak. Often used of a robe of honour

khoja (P.), gentleman, merchant, person of distinction. The usual pronunciation of original *khwaja*

khurjin (P.), saddle-bag. Used as portmanteau

kok (T.), variant of *gök*, q.v.

kuchak (P.), small, minor, junior

kuh (P.), mountain

kumancha (P.), musical instrument like violin

kurt (T.), worm

madrasah (A.), religious school or college. The place where 'lessons' are learnt. A word in use throughout all Muslim countries

manqal (A.), basin to hold burning charcoal

meddah (T.), professional story-teller

mast (P.), thick, boiled milk

mazar (A.), grave, tomb, shrine

mian, miana (P.), centre, middle

mirza (P.), writer, scribe, clerk

mirza-bashi (P. + T.), head-scribe, private secretary

muezzin (PA.), man who sounds the Call to Prayer five times a day for faithful Muslims

mufti (PA.), expounder of the religious law of Islam, 'mufti'

mulla (PA.), learned man, priest

murgh (P.), bird, fowl

Muslim (A.), person professing the faith of Islam; relating to Islam. This word is general throughout the Muslim world

nan (P.), bread

nau (P.), new

nihan- (P.), verbal root denoting settlement

panj (P.), five

paranja (T.), woman's loose dress

pendinka (T.), virulent species of septic ulcer

pulau (T.), savoury rice cooked with fat or butter and served with chicken, meat, etc., embedded in it

-qand, -jand (T.), town, village

qara (T.), black

qara-kurt (T.), 'black worm', large species of spider

qara'ul (T.), observation post, guard, look-out

qaya (T.), rock

qishlaq (T.), winter nomad camp, semi-permanent village

qizil (T.), red

qala (PA.), fort

qum (T.), sand, desert

qumiz (T.), mares' milk

qun (T.), fine of 500 sheep, 50 horses, and 25 camels imposed by Qirghiz on murderer. (Possibly derived from P. *khun,* blood, blood-shedding)

Quran (A.), Muslims' sacred scriptures

qurghan (T.), fort

Qush Begi (T.), Chief Minister

qoyun (T.), sheep

quyu (T.), well (of water)

rabat (A.), rest-house, inn. Pl. *arwat*

rabat-bashi (A. + T.), caretaker of rest-house, innkeeper

rishta (P.), thread; thread-worm, Guinea-worm; v. p. 221

rud (P.), river-bed, river

sai(l) (PA.), flood, torrent

sariq, sari (T.), yellow

Shariah, Shariat (PA.), religious law of Islam based on the Quran and on sacred tradition

Shiah (PA.), large and important sect of Muslims to which most Persians belong

shishlik (T.), strips of meat grilled on a skewer

shams (A.), sun, brightness, glory

shir (P.), lion

shirdil (P.), lion–hearted

Sunni (PA.), orthodox Muslim

surah (A.), chapter of the Quran

surnai (P.), musical reed–pipe

tagh (T.), v. *dagh*

tal (T.), vine

tang (P.), narrow, strait, defile

tapa (T.), hill

tash (T.), 1. stone

2. measure of a short and dignified day's journey

tovarish (R.), comrade

tuman (P.), money of account = 10 qrans (not used in modern Iran). In pre–war years the tuman varied in value between 3s. and 4s. 6d. The word originally meant '10,000', one tuman being supposed to be the equivalent of 10,000 dinars, Arabic silver drachmas

tura (T.), sir, master

tursuq (T.), skin for carrying water, or inflated with air as an aid to swimming

uch (T.), three

ul (A.), the definite article 'the'; v. *al*. Occurs also as *ur-, ush-, ud-*, by assimilation

umara (A), pl. of *amir*, q.v.

urus (T.), Russian, any European

yurt (T.), nomad, semi–permanent tent. Constructed of stout poles set in a circle and covered with felt; v. p. 119

zar (P.), gold

zindan (P.), prison

Other reprints of classic works
available from Ian Faulkner Publishing:

RUSSIAN COURT MEMOIRS
by 'A Russian'
With an introduction by Alan Wood

THE FALL OF THE ROMANOFFS
by '*The Author of Russian Court Memoirs*'
With an introduction by Alan Wood

RUSSIAN PORTRAITS
by Clare Sheridan
Edited by Mark Almond

THE WHITE ARMY
by General A. I. Denikin
With an introduction by Alan Wood

I WAS STALIN'S AGENT
by W. G. Krivitsky
With an introduction by Mark Almond

STALINGRAD
by Heinz Schröter
With an introduction by H. P. Willmott

Full details of these and further publications
may be obtained from:
Ian Faulkner Publishing Ltd
Lincoln House
347 Cherry Hinton Road
Cambridge CB1 4DJ